THE FORCES OF THE OCCULT—
AND WHAT THEY CAN MEAN TO YOU . . .

Here, for the first time, is a *complete* guide to the fascinating—*often personally rewarding*—realm of the occult:

Definitions . . .

Fact . . .

Theory . . .

Explanations . . .

All of the essential terms and phenomenon of Parapsychology—*presented in concise, easy-to-follow form!*

Open the door to the mystery of the occult and discover today the forces which may influence *you!*

AN
OCCULT
DICTIONARY
FOR THE MILLIONS

Howard V. Chambers

AWARD BOOKS
NEW YORK

TANDEM BOOKS
LONDON

Foreword

This dictionary has two essential purposes:

1. It is intended as a guide book and companion for the introductory books on the occult and the paranormal already in print and those projected for future publication in the "For the Millions" series.

2. It is meant to stand on its own as a basic reference work for all those who have discovered the fascination of the paranormal worlds and who may have been put off by the lack of introductory material and by the abundance of terms which seem to have cloudy meanings or meanings on which there is great debate.

Actually, there is nothing terribly difficult about the occult or related subjects; it is only the possibilities for interpreting them which bring confusion. But if we borrow from the example of astrology, we may come to a larger understanding rather quickly and stand a greater chance of making sense of some apparently unrelated information.

For all the guess work and latitude for individual interpretation in astrology, there are certain terms, certain relationships, and certain mathematical factors on which there is universal agreement. An astronomer, for example, might be quite definite in his distaste for the concept of astrology, but he will be forced to accept the astrological uses of the relationships of the planets in the heavens because he uses the *very same* relations in his own discipline.

The use of agreed upon terms is one of the most positive means of bringing the occult, mysterious, and supernatural worlds into sharper focus and for deriving broader benefits from them.

Largely, the intention of this dictionary is that of being informal and interesting. There will be no guide to pronunciation, no references to grammar or parts of speech. In some cases, attempts will be made to pinpoint origins of the words or entries, but only if the origin seems to be of interest.

Abbreviations will be held to an absolute minimum, the most common being q.v., for *quod vide*, Latin for *which see*, used as an indication of a cross reference to a word or term that might bear additional discussion.

Entries in this dictionary will be drawn from widely diverse sources, many of which have already been accepted as sciences. But the occult world is a large one, which frequently overlaps into both formal and informal religions, anthropology, astronomy, biology, medicine, religion, and sociology.

Such a dictionary could not hope to be definitive and all-inclusive in one volume, much less in a volume this size. Yet it is hoped that the excursions taken by this volume, excursions into the Orient, Eastern religions, American Indians, African, New Guinea, and South Pacific peoples as well as folk lore, mythology, and magic will open up and shed more light on previously cloudy worlds.

—Howard V. Chambers

A

AARON—The brother of Moses, his spokesman in Egypt
and the first high priest of the Hebrew religion. Using
him as an agency, Jehovah performed many miracles,
among which was the bursting into flower of a rod
Aaron carried. He was also responsible for the making of
the Golden Calf and the worshipping of it. He appears
in the Old Testament, particularly Deuteronomy, Numbers, and Exodus.

ABADDON—The Hebrew name for Satan, q.v.

ABEDNEGO—In the Bible, he, Meshach, and Shadrach
were taken prisoner by Nebuchadnezzar, king of Babylonia, and cast into a blazing furnace. All three emerged
miraculously unharmed. See Daniel 3:12. Often referred
to by fire walkers and fire handlers, q.v.

ABRACADABRA—A magical formula, used extensively by
early Gnostics to enlist the aid of beneficial spirits in the
warding off of affliction. Also engraved on amulets, q.v.,
to serve as a general protective charm against the forces
of evil. Evolved probably from the Aramaic *abhadda
kedabrah,* "Disappear, O sickness, from this world."

ADAMS, EVANGELINE—American astrologer (1872–1932)
and one of the most widely recognized as having brought
a new dignity to that art. She is famous for a series of
predictions made over a national radio program. The
predictions took place, largely as she had described
them, and the resulting commotion caused her regular
radio program to be cancelled. She is often called the
Mother of Modern Astrology.

AEROMANCY—A form of divination involving the directions of wind. A variation is the throwing of handsful of

7

sand or colored earth into the wind after asking a question and "reading" the answer from the shape of the dust cloud. A further variation is the throwing of a specified number of seeds into the wind and using the resultant pattern, after the seeds have landed, in a manner similar to the reading of tea leaves.

AFFIRMATIONS—A possible forerunner and catalyst of Positive Thinking, q.v. Affirmations are mobilizations of thought, desire, and abilities directed toward the achievement of a specified and worthwhile goal. They are also used to help the individual accept conditions and circumstances he may be temporarily or permanently unable to change. The individual is thus able to channel possible disappointment into constructive activity in areas where he may obtain results. Strikingly similar in intent to White Magic, q.v.

AGAPE—An early form of ritual and spiritual orgy. Derived from the Greek love feast, the agape was clearly erotic in nature and connected with the seasonal fertility rites. By indulging in abandoned eating, drinking, and love making, it was believed that the gods would be pleased and cause good crops, good livestock, and the birth of healthy children.

AGENT—In the occult sense, a living person through whom some form of psychic phenomenon may occur. A medium is an agent through which spiritual forces may communicate. An automatic writer, q.v., is the agent for the transmission of physical messages from the astral world, q.v. Often used interchangeably with control and spiritual guide, both of which see.

AGRIPPA VON NETTESHEIM, HENRY CORNELIUS (1486–1535) A German soldier, physician, alchemist, and astrologer whose reputation survives largely because of his flamboyant, satiric writings which caused many of his contemporaries to become angry with him and to record the fact in their journals. His interest in magic, the occult, and astrology gave him an aura of the mysterious which he did little to discourage. Reputedly, he could see into the future. His predictions, probably based on astrology, were accurate enough to cause him fame. He is said to have found spells and incantations with which he could raise demons, one of which, in the shape of a large black dog, supposedly accompanied him everywhere. Some sources describe a deathbed scene in which he passionately renounced the magical arts in favor of religion. His most famous writing to survive him is *The Occult Philosophy*.

AGLA—A kabbalistic word designed to secure blessing and protection from God, particularly if God's intervention against Satanic forces was required. Like abracadabra, agla found its way onto many kabbalistic scrolls and was worn on amulets. It is a Hebrew acronym for *Athah gabor leolom, Adonai,* "Thou art powerful and eternal, O Lord."

AHOLA—A Hopi Indian kachina, q.v., and representative of the spirit of the Germ God who controls the growth and reproduction of all things. Like other kachinas, this intermediary of the gods appears frequently on earth to assist those who have been faithful in their devotions and sacrifices. At the yearly Hopi Summer Solstice and Bean Dance ceremonies, a man who has undergone ritual purification will wear a white shirt, white kilt, sash, woman's belt, and green moccasins. He will carry a gourd filled with sacred water and also a ceremonial wand. The Hopis believe the spirit of the Germ God will enter this man's body and dictate his movements in the ceremonial dances.

Aío—A Hopi Indian spiritual guide who assists mortals when they wish to contact the gods.

AKASHIC RECORDS—A somewhat fatalistic Eastern approach to the Book of Life concept. In these cosmic records "all that ever was *is*," and "all that will ever be *is.*" They contain the complete activities of every being who ever lived or who will ever live. Some seers and prophets have supposedly found the means to gain access to these records, hence their abilities at prediction. An individual who is able to "tune in" on the records may not be able to avail himself of all the information they contain. This indicates some spiritual advancement, but by no means the maximum degree. Implicit in the concept of the records is the fact that they may not be used for any purposes of self-gain other than that of spiritual advancement. They are of particular significance to many religions and philosophies which accept the possibility of reincarnation, q.v., since a spiritually adept individual may consult these records, discover what his past lives were and how he behaved in them, then determine which karmic debts he is working off and how he can best pay attention to these. See also KARMA.

AMANITA MUSCARARIA—Circles of white-stalked, red-capped fungus; often called "fairy rings," they are even more popularly known as "fly agaric." Closely related to another fungus, the deadly "destroying angel," this is a growth which contains a powerful alkaloid, used in provoking intense, long-lasting hallucinations. It is particularly well used in Central and Northeastern Siberia, where primitive peasants seem to have known of its properties for hundreds of years. It is frequently imported into North America and Europe and is well known in connection with the ceremonial mushroom of Mexico and with the current interest in psychedelics, both of which see.

AMON-RA—The Egyptian spirit of the four elements: air, water, fire, and earth.

AMULET—A charm or token worn or carried on the person. Generally, there are two classes of amulets: those resembling fetishes, q.v., and being the dwelling place of spirits; those which have shapes, inscriptions, designs, etc. which ward off evil spirits and bad fortune or black magic.

Amulets have been traced back to primitive man and woman, who wore or carried such items as sea shells, chunks of rock or wood which had a pleasing or unusual appearance to them. As men became more sophisticated in their awareness of spirits, magic, spells, incantations, etc., they began attributing special protective or healing qualities to various elements and mottoes. This aspect was furthered by the development of clans, q.v., moieties, q.v., and secret societies, which had special symbols and charms.

A variation of the amulet is the medicine bag carried by American Indians, containing bits of rock, wood, animal hide, bones, etc. and which served the same purpose as the amulet. In some cases, the medicine bag was simply a convenience for carrying the charmed items, but the bag and amulet cases—a box of precious metal, a bag of cloth or leather—also had the advantage of keeping the contents free from the contamination of evil spirits, the evil eye, or of persons considered uninitiated in the matters of ritual magic and, thus, suspicious in nature.

ANALEPTICS—Drugs which produce the opposite effect of a sedative are called analeptics; these are characterized by responses of super action and movement, causing stimulation and arousal. They are popularly believed to stimulate and increase mental activity without producing the hallucinatory effects of psychedelics. Experimentally used in supervised drug therapy situations, they have been administered in conjunction with LSD-25, q.v. Examples of analeptics are benzedrene and cocaine.

ANGELS—Beings of either sex, created by God or elevated to their position by intelligence or spiritual advancement and composed of heavenly matter. Different religions ascribe different functions to them, but generally speaking, their purpose is good; their duties consist of performing heavenly tasks or assisting humans in matters of spiritual enlightenment. Some are spoken of as intermediaries between the God-force and mortals, while to others are ascribed such protective functions as watching over entire nations and races of man. They may appear in some recognizable fleshly form or may remain invisible. They generally have powers of flight, rapid travel, and the abilities to perform functions that men would consider miracles.

Fallen angels are those who possess the same miraculous abilities, but who have fallen out of favor with God. They seem to have allied themselves with Satan and will perform functions which range from moderately evil to completely and instinctively evil. As opposed to their higher counterparts, they seem to exist for the purpose of doing evil and encouraging evil.

ANGLE—In astronomy, any of the four Cardinal Points of an horoscope. These points fall in the signs of Aries, Cancer, Libra, and Capricorn. They are called the Cardinal Signs. They represent the first, fourth, seventh, and tenth houses of the zodiac and a planet is said to be angular when it falls in one of these.

ANIMA—The spiritual force. The soul and spirit found in all living things. It is variously considered the presence of God in all living things, the life-force in all living things and the vital, life-sustaining force of the universe. Many consider it a spiritual fuel of all life, in all realms of the universe.

ANKH—The Egyptian symbol of the life of the soul after physical death. It represents the union of male and female principles and is supposedly the source from which soul and anima spring. One of the most powerful of all Egyptian symbols, it is generally found accompanying illustrations of the deities, often in combination with the Dad and Tat symbols, both of which see.

ANTHROPOMANCY—A form of divination in which the entrails of a specially sacrificed human being are used to read omens and portents of the future. This practice is rather ancient and is confined almost exclusively to civilizations which practiced other forms of human sacrifice. Exceptions are African tribes which use this practice when an individual has been killed by an animal.

In more recent times, various primitive peoples have modified this custom by using entrails of freshly killed animals. The length, form, and conditions of the organs influenced the "reading" which was usually performed by a priest or witch doctor.

In cases involving human sacrifice, pieces of the entrails were often used as powerful good luck charms, after the "reading" had been made.

ANTIDOTES—A remedy or cure for a curse or spell; a counteraction to the ingestion of a philtre or herb concoction. In any civilization, primitive or sophisticated, so long as there were spells and curses and potions, there were possibilities of antidotes or counterspells from stronger sources. Antidotes were dispensed and sold by witch doctors, sorcerers, alchemists, apothecaries, good spirits, and evil spirits. Although antidotes often involved nonorganic charms, they often also involved portions of animals. But most frequently, they were composed of herbs and probably evolved through the fact that women were forced to have a thorough knowledge of herbs, barks, plants, etc. for food and for treatment of minor injuries.

Antidotes often became a matter of a contest between two or more witch doctors, shamans, or midwives, the contest being to see who could evolve the most powerful potion for which there was no remedy. More often than not, this worked to the great disadvantage of an unsuspecting victim.

APOTHECARIES—Galen, who ranks next to Hippocrates in the lexicon of physicians, was one of the first physicians to evolve complex prescriptions for the cure of disease and ailments. Often, his therapeutics became so involved that a hundred or more elements were needed for the curing potion. While many doctors who followed Galen's methods kept their own store of drugs and herbs, some were too busy and took to writing out prescriptions which the patient might have filled by midwives, retired prostitutes, and quack healers. The first apothecary or drug shops were groceries, where the drugs and herbs were kept as a sideline, but as the success of Galen's theories spread, both quacks and reputable chemists opened stores devoted entirely to the sale of medications, ointments, herbs, and the filling of prescriptions on order from physicians.

APPARITION—From its Latin derivation, this term means the appearance of a paranormal phenomenon. Often used interchangeably with ghost, poltergeist, and even visions of the future. But it should be reserved for the description of any visible object of supernatural origin. Apparitions are not necessarily limited to living things; they may include materializations of inanimate objects. See APPORTS. They may include astral bodies, formerly living beings and animals. A famous example of an apparition is the ghost of Hamlet's father, visible to Hamlet but to none of the other characters.

Primitive societies consider dreams as well as drug-induced reveries to be apparitions, particularly if the dreamer sees images of the dead, who make predictions which are later fulfilled.

The most common concept of an apparition is that of a being returning from the dead to accomplish some deed.

The production of ectoplasm, q.v., or some visible form by a medium may be considered to be an apparition.

APPOLONIUS OF TYANA—A Greek philosopher, and contemporary of Christ, who studied mathematics with Pythagoras and who was reputed to have magical powers which he used in healing sick individuals and for transforming elements at will. Some of the behavior attributed to him indicates activities very much on the order of a modern researcher of psychic phenomena. Because of his apparent ability to recognize witches and vampires, and because of his ability to emerge unscathed from a plague-infested area, a great deal of myth has sprung up about his magical abilities. He reportedly did not die a physical death but was, instead, plucked from the earth in a manner similar to the divine enlightenment he preached. In this theory, an individual, at the moment of his highest spiritual development, merges with the God-power of the astral world.

APPORTS—One of the many controversial words in the occult field, apports are accepted by many persons as being objects which actually materialize through the agency of a physical medium. Other sources say apports are already present and are merely used to indicate the presence of invisible spirits who are unable to materialize further. The apports produced by many reputable physical mediums seem to suggest that these objects actually materialize during the course of a seance. Some theories suggest apports are transported from other earthly locations to the site of the seance by spirit messengers, part of whose duties are to help convince mortals of the spiritual world.

Reported examples of apports include rattling tambourines, tooting horns, shrilling whistles, the appearance of flowers, fruit, coins, and small animals. Another apport is the presence of a perfumed scent.

More than any other form of seance phenomena, apports are looked upon with suspicion because of the possibility of trickery and because of the show business nature of their appearance. A suggested and workable definition for apports: Items which are brought to a seance by a nonpartial individual who has no connection with the medium and which may be mobilized into action during the course of the seance by means which are obviously not mechanical or human in nature.

AQUARIUS—In astrology, the water bearer. Eleventh sign of the zodiac, q.v. It is an airy, moist, rational, humane sign, the day-house of the planet Saturn. The native is above average in height and often robust. This sign rules the legs and ankles, causing such diseases that will affect either. Its colors are sky blue and grey.

ARIES—In astrology, the house of Mars. A commanding sign, its colors are red and white. Its native will be warm, hasty, and passionate. It is the First House of the zodiac, q.v.

ARUSPEX—Fortune telling and divination from the formation of birds in flight. Factors involved are the type of bird, the number in the formation, the direction of flight, and the time of day at which the flight is noticed.

ASCENDANT—In astrology, a measurement of degree between a planet and the Eastern horizon at the moment of an individual's birth. Often referred to as the rising sign.

ASPECT—In astrology, a series of angular relationships which may exist between the planets. Most astrologers consider favorable relationships or aspects to occur when specific planets are sextile, or 60 degrees apart, and trine, when the planets are 120 degrees apart. See GRAND TRINE.

Unfavorable aspects occur when two specific planets are square, or 90 degrees apart, and in opposition, 180 degrees apart. Astrologers may also consider conjunction—two planets in the same sign of the zodiac at the same time—to be an aspect, but opinion varies on whether this is favorable or unfavorable.

ASTARTE—The Semitic goddess of fertility, beauty, and love; she is sometimes referred to as the goddess of the moon. She appears in the Bible as Ashtaroth and is the most important of all Phoenecian goddesses, corresponding to the Greek Aphrodite and the Babylonian Ishtar.

ASTRAL BODY—A spiritual essence and intelligence allegedly present in all human beings. It is composed of matter which is much finer than the ordinary physical body. It may penetrate the physical body and be partially or wholly detached from it. In the astral body are passions, emotions, and most desires, along with the ability to feel. These qualities are returned to the physical body only with the return of a departed astral body.

Some dreams are said to be impressions of astral flights, in which the astral body detaches itself from the physical host for some mission. Examples of this sort of behavior are interpreted variously. One such explanation describes the case of a person dreaming of a distant friend who brings a warning of impending danger. Upon awakening and investigating, the danger is discovered to be real and a subsequent check with the individual dreamed of reveals that this person had some impression of trouble and wished to warn about it.

Thus, the detachment of the astral body from the physical body does not necessarily imply physical death or a subsequent inability to return. During the detachment, the astral body may remain invisible or become an apparition, assuming the exact physical properties and characteristics of the host body. It may cause itself to be seen in opaque or translucent states by other mortals. There is a possibility of astral bodies being mistaken for ghosts.

The astral body may become detached through conscious projection, through subconscious desire, and as a result of physical or psychic accidents.

When detachment occurs, the body is able to navigate in the physical and astral world.

ASTRAL WORLD—The second lowest of the seven worlds, both of which are supposedly the only two able to be understood with any clarity by mortals. It is the world directly beyond that of physical life.

At the death of the physical being, the astral body moves into the astral world, where it is given the opportunity for further advancement, either by performing various deeds of assistance and importance or by developing a more spiritual approach to the higher worlds above. It is commonly believed that the more highly civilized a man is at the time of his death, the more time he will need in the astral world.

Some sources cite descriptions of the astral world and the one directly ahead of it, having been transmitted by spirits inhabiting this world. Most of such material is doubtful, tends to be ambiguous, and varies considerably from source to source.

The astral world is opened to and has been inhabited temporarily by living men, some of whom were religious adepts and others versed in the occult. Particularly among seventeenth and eighteenth century occultists, persons who "disappeared" for significant lengths of time and refused to talk about their lives during this period were assumed to have moved bodily into the astral world. These persons, of course, did little to discourage such beliefs.

Some persons have stumbled into the astral world by the process of "involuntary" astral projection and have developed the ability to return at will.

Clairvoyants are said to move in this sphere while seeking information of the future and it is this area more than any other where spiritualists make their contacts at seances.

Although the astral world is a Theosophical concept, many mystic and primitive religions seem to have counterparts of it. To cite brief examples of the potential for comparison; the Hindu mystics, Sri Ramakrishna and Swami Vivikenanda, may have entered the astral world in their various ecstasies or illuminations, bringing back with them the wisdom and composure to assist them in being exemplary religious leaders.

ASAFETIDA BAG—Foul-smelling gum resin obtained from the members of the carrot family. Because of the foul smell, quantities of the substance were worn about the neck as a part of an amulet to keep disease and evil spirits away. Used by some alchemists, apothecaries, and physicians as an anticonvulsant, this led all the more toward the belief that the more foul and penetrating the smell, the more effective a charm or medicine.

ASTROLOGY—An ancient practice, probably started in Babylon about 3,000 years ago and regarded by many moderns as a science. Although the majority of modern scientists consider it a pseudo-science and a sham, it is winning a great number of adherents because of the accuracy of its predictions. Because of a great similarity to the science of astronomy, at least in the matter of mathematics and planetary positions, it is regarded as the most likely of the occult areas to gain scientific acceptance.

Basically, astrology is a means of divination and interpretation based on the division of the heavens into twelve equal parts, called the zodiac, q.v., and attributing to these parts characteristics which are determined by the positions of planets in the heavens. Thus, each equal part of the zodiac, or house, is ruled by a particular planet. Persons born at the time of rule by a particular planet may be said to have unique characteristics.

By working out horoscopes, which are detailed maps of the heavens at the time of an individual's birth, certain inferences may be drawn about personality, character, profession, talents, and desires.

There are different branches of astrology, including those which deal with the prospects for nations and organizations. Another branch deals with weather predictions.

Many modern astrologers believe that astrology will

gain more acceptance if it is regarded more as an art than as a science. They maintain that their mathematics are as indisputable as the mathematics of astronomy, provided they are given correct data. The schism between astrology and astronomy falls largely in the matter of divination. And it is this area of interpretation which modern astrologers feel should make their work more an art than a science, since some intuitiveness is seemingly required.

It is doubtful exactly when astrology first came into prominence, but certainly among the first practitioners was Hermes Trismegistus, or Thoth, who, under various names, gave revelations to mortals for writing down. So far as mortals are concerned, the name of Ptolemy, the Egyptian mathematician and map maker, stands out. Modern astrologers of note include Evangeline Adams, James Clancy, Robert De Luce, and Carl Payne Tobey. (For further discussion of astrology, see ZODIAC, HOUSES OF. See also, *An Astrology Primer for the Millions* by Carl Payne Tobey.)

ATARAXIA—Greek for a state of mental serenity combined with physical well-being. In current usage, an ataraxic is a drug which tranquilizes without producing sleep. A good example of an ataraxic is Miltown (Meprobamate). In occult lore, ataraxia was a valuable and desired state before attempting to enter into communication with the gods or spiritual forces.

ATLANTIS—A continent which supposedly existed in the area now occupied by the Atlantic ocean and which was destroyed by a violent series of earthquakes, volcanic eruptions, and tidal waves. It has been a topic of discussion for thousands of years and proponents of its existence have made much of the fact that it was mentioned by Plato, who claimed that the Atlanteans overran Europe and would have conquered all of it, had it not been for a successful counteroffensive by the Greeks.

Amateur archeologists are, from time to time, producing potsherds or other artifacts which they offer as proof that there was a complex, well-developed Atlantean civilization, capable of greater feats than even the Mayans. At present, there is no evidence to substantiate the theory of Atlantis except some imaginative interpretations of ancient writings and scriptures and the claims of some spiritualists who offer as evidence contacts made with former Atlanteans, now in the spirit world.

Geologists and geographers, operating within the scientific framework of probability, are perhaps more charitable than other scientists who say Atlantis is a totally absurd concept. The geologists who care to comment on the subject say there is no probability that Atlantis ever existed ... nor is there any evidence that it did not exist.

Probable or not, the fact remains that Atlantis has a sister continent, in the occult realm if not in reality. It is the Pacific continent of Mu, q.v., or Lemuria.

ATMAN—In Hindu religions, the supreme spirit or soul; a universal soul or source of all souls. It is generally monotheistic in concept and more often popular with individuals who do not need an anthropomorphic or manlike god. Due to the wide divergence of Hindu sects—which greatly outnumber Christian sects—atman has been endowed with different meanings and has been the source of many schisms. Many agree on this much: Atman is a form of spiritual awareness of soul arrived at through ritual purification, study, and deed. It is a force to be recognized by the individual, studied, then achieved.

AURA—An emanation which is believed by occultists to surround the physical body in a cloudlike light, composed of layers of color. Supposedly, this aura is present at all times, but is rarely visible except to those who are advanced in some form of occultism, such as clairvoyance, mediumship, etc. Both Christian and Hindu religious figures are often portrayed with auras, particularly about the head, and it is said that certain religious personalities have had such powerful auras that they were more likely visible to the pious.

The theosophist view of the aura is that it contains five specific layers or divisions, the color of each a key to the specific nature of a facet of personality. The divisions are: the health aura, the vital aura, the karmic aura, the character aura, and the aura of the individual's spiritual nature.

The colors which may tint or dominate these layers and their approximate meanings are as follows: rose=affection; brilliant red=anger or force; muddy red =passion and the sensual; yellow=the intellectual activities; orange=pride and ambition; purple=spirituality, occult power, and psychic ability; blue=religiousness; green=jealousy and deceit.

These colors may all merge with one another, signifying varying degrees of the qualities they portray.

AUTOMATIC WRITING—Written messages which are transmitted from spirits or beings in the astral world or beyond to living persons, and transmitted through a spiritual control or directly, when the living person has experience.

The recipient of the automatic message may perform the writing in or out of trance; examples of each have been discussed at length.

Many cases of involuntary automatic writing exist. The recipient seems to be seized by an irrepressible desire to take up pen or pencil and paper. After doing so, a message comes forth purporting to be from a spiritual agency.

Tests similar to those employed to ascertain the truthfulness of seance-received messages have been attempted with automatic writing. The results are varied, but there are a significant number of cases involved when individuals wrote down intimate details, descriptions, and other knowledge they could not possibly have known from any natural source.

Messages received by automatic writers have also appeared in foreign languages, some quite obscure, and backwards, so that the final message had to be held before a mirror in order to be read.

There seems to be no set time in life when those adept at automatic writing have begun receiving messages; some start quite early, others seem to have repressed the urge for years.

In spite of considerable experiments performed by the Society for Physical Research and other sincere investigators of psychic phenomena, automatic writing often comes under critical fire. It is often difficult to check the conditions under which the writing is performed, there is a strong atmosphere of a party game attached and it is possible that the writer may simply be seeking attention as a psychic adept.

Nevertheless, there have been astounding results, a good example of which is a message received by a medium-writer while in a trance. The sender of the message identified himself by name and the handwriting of the medium-writer was checked against samples of handwriting from the alleged sender of the message. Not only did the medium's handwriting closely resemble the handwriting style of the departed and differ markedly from the medium's normal handwriting, the message used characteristic misspellings and punctuation of the deceased.

AVICI—A form of hell described by Theosophists. It is interesting to compare avici with the astral world. In it, an individual remains after death in exactly the same physical entity he had before physical death. He is subject to the cravings, desires, and appetites felt in the physical world, but in avici, he is totally unable to experience the satisfaction of these desires. The individual may work himself out of avici after an indeterminate stay.

B

BA—In Egyptian religion, a concept similar to anima. It is the soul or life force, but also contains particles of the essence of the gods. It is depicted as a bird with the head of a man and is most often seen in illustration as being near a mummy case. One of its major functions is to visit a mummy from time to time, bringing to it comfort and assurances of immortality. It is often represented as carrying the ankh, q.v.

BAAL—A term used in the old testament for the gods of Canaan. See MOLOCH.

BACABS—Four Mayan gods who stood at each corner of the world and held it up. Their names were Kan, Muluc, Ix, Cuac. They also symbolized the directions of east, north, west, and south, respectively, and were gods of rain and agriculture.

BACHELOR—One of several names given Satan on the occasion of his appearance on earth in the form of a goat, during which times he participated in the ritual sexual orgy with witches.

BACCHUS—In Greek and Roman mythology, he was the god of wine and also the equivalent of Dionysus, q.v. The Romans called him Liber on occasion, but held fairly often to Bacchus. His favor could be enlisted through the simple expedient of drinking wine and he was thought to be particularly beneficial to persons who were quite drunk. At this time, he provided a greater sexual capacity and tended to help ward off evil spells.

BALOI—Mythical beings who scavenge graves for useful

parts of corpses, which are then used for nourishment or for power to enforce spells of black magic.

BANSHEE—An Irish apparition, the spirit of a female or a being with a female personality. Two distinct beliefs are current concerning the meaning and function of the Banshee. One holds that she is the possession of a specific family line, appearing to announce the death of one of their number. She is had only by families of pure stock and will not concern herself with families in which there is any Norman, Saxon, or Angle stock.

The other point of view holds that she is available to all, and that to hear her wail, even if she is announcing the death of another, is a signal of impending tragedy.

Both points of view agree that she may be somewhat malevolent and cause a commotion similar to that of a poltergeist, q.v. Also, both beliefs agree that the hearing of a banshee giving a low, sweet-sounding wail is an omen of a gentle death and a prospect of speedy redemption. An angry, determined wail from her bodes for a grim death and a poor prospect of heaven.

She may or may not be visible to accomplish her mission, but she is reputedly always visible to the specific individual on whom she waits.

BENEMMERINNEN—Hebrew witches who haunt women in childbirth for the purpose of stealing new infants.

BENGE—An oracle poison found in Africa, particularly among the Azande. It is a red paste, related to strychnine, but considered to be a supernatural agent. When fed to an animal for the purpose of divination, benge does not kill because of its toxicity, rather because of a willingful decision to do so ... or not to do so. This last is important because the medicine man who administers the poison to an animal must give the poison all relevant details of the issue to be solved, in such a way that the matter may be decided by a yes or no answer. Thus, the poison administered to an animal may either kill it or not, and present two clear-cut answers for the question at hand.

A noted anthropologist studying the benge poison oracle reports that it kills about half the animals to which it is given, but for no apparent reason. Neither the amount of the poison nor the health of the animal seem related to the animal's survival. See POISON ORACLES.

BEELZEBUB—Used interchangeably as Satan, any devil, or a devil of particularly high powers. John Milton used him in his famed poem, *Paradise Lost*, as Satan's chief lieutenant, which seems to have given the name that definition for current use.

BERSERK—From Norse legend, a warrior who worked himself into a religious frenzy before battle. Considered a form of divine protection from injury and, should death result, the berserk state was supposedly strong enough to elevate the slain warrior into heaven. Interesting comparison with certain Japanese soldiers of the Shinto belief during World War II, and the Hindu followers of Juggernaut, the eighth avatar of Vishnu, q.v., whose idol at Puri, India, is drawn on a heavy cart under the wheels of which frenzied devotees are alleged to have thrown themselves.

BISBA—A modern method of reading the character and personality of women by size, shape, and other configuratory measurements of the breast. This method is predicated on the belief that the woman's breast reveals more of her character, whether surpressed or expressed, than any other means.

BLACK MAGIC—The use of supernatural forces for the purpose of evil. The main directions of this negative art seem to be a perversion of all mortality and the desecration of all laws of benevolent gods or charms.

Black magic may be employed for personal gain, for

revenge, or to "enlist" another individual into the ranks of Satanic forces.

There are three basic approaches to its practice: divination, bewitchment, and necromancy. By use of spells, incantations, and supernatural powers granted by the dark forces, an individual may cause the illness of an individual, death, destruction, or even the transmutation of animate and inanimate objects.

Connected strongly with Black Magic are unusual sexual practices, ranging from the deliberate defloration of innocent virgins to sexual activities between evil and mischievous spirits and sleeping humans. See INCUBUS and SUCCUBUS.

Participation in these rites is said to celebrate the black and dark powers and to strengthen these arts in mortals. Strange sexual activity is often used to lure innocents into the ranks of the malevolent by causing the primitive sides of their natures to dominate the more civilized.

BLACK MASS—A black magic ritual in which the forces of evil are appeased and given devotion. Often, a good portion of this mass is a direct parody of or attempt to desecrate the Christian concept of mass and sacraments. In it, the Lord's Prayer is recited backwards and homage is paid Satan. Toasts are drunk in blood, human victims may be sacrificed or tortured, and excessive sexual conduct is encouraged. Demons and witches are the chief participants, and often the occasion of the Black Mass is the Witches' Sabbath, q.v.

BLARNEY STONE, THE—Irish legend has it that there is a large stone in a castle at the village of Blarney, County Cork. About twenty feet from the top of a wall and accessible only with great difficulty, the stone reputedly has magical powers which may be transmitted to the person who kisses it. His reward: the gift of easy and beautiful speech.

BLAVATSKY, HELENA—(1831–1891) A spiritualist known more popularly as Madam Blavatsky. After an early experience with seances and mysticism, she became a convert of occultism. She read and studied the subject copiously, then attempted to enter Tibet for further training in the mystic arts. Nothing is known of the time she spent in her studies there, but in 1870 she returned to civilization and traveled to America. Here, she became prominent in occult circles, particularly as a medium. She formed a mixture of theosophy, q.v., and Eastern mysticism into a package and attempted to gain a following. Decidedly on the evangelical side, she soon attracted over 100,000 faithful followers. Her main premise seems to have been the combination of her spiritualist control elements with Buddhistic legends. She claimed to have direct astral communication with two Tibetan mahatmas.

Many adverse reports exist, describing with skepticism the "psychic miracles" she performed to convince potential converts of her occult adeptness.

BLINDFOLDING—As an occult practice, this was done either as a preventative or to enhance certain powers. Many primitive tribes in Africa, New Guinea, and in the Pacific Islands will blindfold corpses before burial or cremation. This is done to prevent the spirit from returning to haunt the living.

In certain instances, animals and birds are blindfolded, particularly at the time they are hatching eggs or rearing young. This is believed to make the offspring adept at pointing out locations of gold or of sacred plants or of herbs useful in concocting potions.

BOOK OF THE DEAD, THE—A mystical Egyptian work dealing with the preparation of the soul for transformation into the spiritual world. It is supposedly read by the living against the time when they will be embalmed as mummies. Various incantations are offered to assist the soul in strengthening its powers of perception and development so that, on the Day of Judgment, it will be of sufficient weight to merit being saved.

The incantations are highly mystical in order and concern the opening of the senses to various experiences.

Because of these incantations and the discussions of spiritual experience, the book is finding great currency with certain users of LSD-25 and other psychedelics, q.v., the theory being that *The Book of the Dead* is an adjunct to the consciousness expanding properties of these drugs and of the mystical-religious experiences which might be felt under their influence.

BONE POINTING—A form of ritual black magic practiced by tribes in Africa, Haiti, New Guinea, and Australia. The victim is confronted by an adversary who points at him an animal bone which has been given potence by a witch doctor. Victims of this magic often become so resigned to the lethal effects that they refuse help and food; they take to their huts and await death. Only the rapid administration of an effective countercharm or antidote can save them from death by fear and despair.

One tribe, the Murngin of Australia, are so conditioned to the lethal effects of bone pointing that the moment the event takes place, the entire community begins an elaborate funeral ritual, which takes death for granted and hopes to speed the soul of the victim on to the spirit world in peace.

The one drawback of bone pointing is the fee paid to the witch doctor for an effective bone. If the charm is not powerful enough, the victim may return to haunt the adversary after his own death.

BROWNIES—A household spirit of Scotland origin. They are male, small, with wrinkled faces, short, curly brown hair, and long nosed. They are brown in dress and tawny in complexion. Their job is to protect a house from strange spirits, and while they expect no pay nor recognition in the form of offerings or sacrifices, it is said of them that they are not adverse to a bowl of cream and a slice of bread, which should be left for them in such a manner as to appear accidental. Essentially friendly in nature, their one bit of mischief is a fondness for stealing cream and bread crusts.

BUDDHA—The enlightened one. The name applied to Gautama Siddhartha, a religious philosopher who lived in India at approximately 563-483 B.C, and who began a religious practice which has spread from India into China, Japan, and portions of Asia. The name is also applied to adepts in the religion, persons who have divine wisdom and virtue.

BUNE—One of the most powerful demons of the infernal regions and a lieutenant of Satan. His only visible form is that of a man, but he does not speak. He haunts tombs and cemeteries and leads other demons around places of death. Those who recognize and serve him are given grand powers of persuasiveness, but an intimate knowledge of demonology is required before he will pass time with any mortal.

BULL ROARER—Found in Africa, the South Pacific, and New Guinea, this is a form of whistle which may be carved from wood or rock and either thrown into the air or spun about the head on a tether. In either case, it produces a low, eerie moan and is used to represent the voice of various gods or spirits. Its use is almost exclusively for male clan members while engaged in ritual magic ceremonies. Women are traditionally supposed to be ignorant of its existence and actually fear the sound as they would fear the gods. A woman is supposed to die immediately if she discovers what the bull roarer is.

The male clan members, after employing the bull roarer, supposedly have the appropriate gods present to listen to their needs and to help prepare them for further ritual.

BURIAL PRACTICES—From culture to culture, these vary from cremation and inurnment to ritual cannibalism and mummification. But nearly all magic believing cultures perform some act which will help insure that the spirit does not return to earth for any purpose motivated by anger and revenge. The primitives want their contacts with spirits to be confined to friendly, benevolent beings and will thus make sacrifices, blindfold corpses, make idols and images and, in some cases, mutilate portions of their own bodies.

In nearly all primitive burial practices, some provision is made against desecration of the grave by other humans or by evil spirits, since it is believed that the spirit of a desecrated corpse may return to haunt his family or clan until some rite is performed which will help the departed gain entry into the spirit world.

The burning of plants, incense, and other offerings as well as the burial of the dead with protective amulets help insure these ends.

C

CAAPI—A natural hallucinogenic agent, q.v., which is used in ritual debauches by the Indians of Peru, Colombia, Ecuador, and Brazil. Known since the time of Cortez, it is also drunk by medicine men prior to settling disputes, casting spells, or reading the future. Due to the hallucinations and expanded consciousness aspects of the drug, it is thought to have great supernatural powers, enabling a medicine man to read the future, communicate with the gods, and ingest in his own body a portion of the god-like substance.

CACTUS TREE WORSHIP—Popular among African peoples who believe certain trees in the cactus family possess souls from which the human race sprang. The tree is venerated in much the same way as a white cow in India among the Hindus.

CACODEMON—An evil spirit who was quite agile in changing his shape and appearance. He was supposedly one of two spirits assigned to every mortal, the cacodemon representing the genius of the evil impulse. Some astrologers, particularly the ancients, regard the twelfth house of the sun, which has evil properties, that of the cacodemon.

CADUCEUS—The staff carried by the Greek God Hermes; a winged staff about which were twined two serpents. Both the wings and the serpents gave this staff a powerful magic, making it swift, potent, and of a healing nature. Hermes later gave this staff to Aesculapius, a man who was probably a mortal but who became deified as the god of medicine. It is quite common to see the caduceus used today as a sign related to modern medicine, but at one time, the sight of it was said to have the same effect on disease, plague, and sickness that the cross had on vampires and werewolves.

CAGLIOSTRO—(1743–1795) A Sicilian alchemist and perhaps the most famed occult figure of all time, he was born Guiseppe Balsamo, and through a series of ruses, blackmailings, predictions, and writings, secured for himself the title of a count. He has attracted the interest of such famed writers as Thomas Carlyle, and precisely because so very much was written about him, it is difficult to compare sources and give an accurate account. As is the case with almost every such legendary figure, accounts of his activities became distorted and embellished.

In many senses, he bears a strong career resemblance to the more modern spiritualist, Eusapia Palladino, inasmuch as he could probably perform some occult feats which defied definition or explanation. But he was given to a good deal of mischief and had expensive tastes. On various pretexts of transmuting base elements into gold or regenerating the physical bodies of the elderly, he extracted great sums of money.

His most ambitious project seems to have been the organization of his Egyptian Masonic Rite Temple, which admitted both men and women—but to separate temples—and sold them costumes, gave exhibitions of occult magic, had classes instructing the initiates, and did everything possible to offer background and pageantry in the mystical and occult.

Although Cagliostro was widely read and his publications sold at great prices, his best talent seems to have been in extracting money from people in a manner that was instructive to them if not enjoyable.

CAKE, WORTHINGTON—An Irish occultist who embodied many of Cagliostro's techniques in his own late eighteenth century Society of the Mystic Spiral. In Ireland, England, and the United States, Cake presented lavish seances, demonstrations of levitation and mesmerism, and based an elaborate system of communication with the spirit world and reincarnation on the principle of the spiral. He claimed the physical world was likened to the outer ring of the spiral. As an individual progressed spiritually, he moved to a progressively smaller circle in the giant spiral, ultimately reaching a point of infinity, at which time he merged with the supreme spiritual force.

CALENDAR OF LUCKY AND UNLUCKY DAYS, THE—Composed by the Egyptian magician, Leti, this calendar had a strong similarity to astrology in that it attempted to predict what day and hour would be most propitious for any given undertaking.

The British Museum in London has a complete copy of this remarkable document, which divided the day into three basic parts and based predictions on the powers of the various gods which presided over these aspects.

CALLIOPE—Daughter of Zeus and Mnemosyne; one of the nine muses, q.v. Represented as holding a tightly rolled parchment, Calliope is the muse of epic poetry and is said to grant special favors and inspirations to those involved in the composition of such poems.

CANAC—One of four Mayan gods who held up the earth. See BACABS.

CANCER—In astrology, the sign of the crab and the fourth house of the zodiac, q.v. It is the only house of the moon and the colors ruled by it are green and russet. Its natives are fair and pale, short and small.

CANNABIS—Indian hemp family, which includes bahang, hashish, ganja, and marihuana. The dried flowering tops of the female plants are smoked, or extracts and resins are taken orally. In Hindu tradition, it is regarded as a holy plant, brought from the ocean by the god Shiva. It is regarded by some Mohammedan sects as an embodiment of the spirit of the prophet. It produces euphoria, excitement, temporal and spatial distortion, and hallucinations.

CANNIBALISM, RELIGIOUS—Feasting on the flesh of a human being in the belief that the properties of the victim—his skills, powers, physical strength, bravery, or knowledge—will be imparted. Also employed if the victim has amassed material possessions in his lifetime or if he is young and the qualities of his youth are desired.

CAPRICORN—In astrology, the sign of the goat and the house of Saturn. The native is supposedly slender in stature, cheerful and collected in disposition. See ZODIAC.

CAT'S EYE—A semi-precious stone used as a protection against the evil eye, q.v., and to assure the wearer a long life.

CASSANDRA—The daughter of Priam, king of Troy, who appealed to the god Apollo for the gift of prophecy in return for her favors. The gift was granted and her ability as a seeress was unquestioned, but when the time came for Cassandra to give herself to Apollo, she refused. The angered god had given her such complete and extensive powers of prophecy that even he was unable to take them away from her, but in retaliation, he provided that all who heard her predictions would refuse to believe them.

CAYCE, EDGAR—An early twentieth century American who became a psychic physician, q.v. While in a trance state, he was able to offer amazing powers of diagnosis and prescription for individuals in his presence or for individuals who had written to him for advice. He never charged for this service and often gave prescriptions which involved materia medica which were no longer common. Returning to a trance state, Cayce would tell his patient exact locations of the missing ingredient so that his prescription could be compounded accurately. He had an amazing percentage of cures to his credit.

CHALK, MAGIC—Rubbed on the forehead to increase intelligence and provide ability to see into the future. The chalk is given its powers by a magician, who places it under the severed head of a dead person, where it supposedly absorbs the essence which drips down from the brain.

CHANGELING—In Scotland, a belief in the substitution of a little mannekin of the elf race in the place of a human child. Although old in age and spirit, the mannekin is given the same physical appearance as the child. It grows up with a cranky personality, is frequently misshapen, particularly about the face and, in general, plagues the parents and others about him. It may be of any sex and is removed by stabbing, dropping into a river, or forcing him to sit on an oven. Supposedly, the original child will be returned if the changeling is discovered in time. But accounts of the changeling myth give no definite clues to the fate of the child or the possibility of his recovery.

CHARMS—A magical formula, written, sung, or recited over an amulet or talisman, q.v., in order to provide potency for some beneficial result. This is the preferred use of the word, since the context of certain inanimate objects and bits of human hair, skin, bones, etc. and animal matter may be considered to be covered in the definitions of amulets, fetishes, talismans, etc.

CHARMS, BURNT—Special formulas or prayers which would be written on paper, leaves, etc. and burned, thus offering them to the gods, sanctifying them, and protecting them from contamination by other spirits. Numerous occasions exist in which a medicine man will instruct the patient to use the written charm as a wrapping for a cigarette or cigar. Burned over a fire, the fumes may be inhaled, or the ashes may be mixed with water or other solutions and drunk. Many of these prayers and formulas are centuries old.

CHELIDONUS—A Gaelic and Celtic folk remedy which has also found its way into North America. It is a small stone found in a bird, which must be killed. It is considered great fortune to find such a stone and is used as a cure against melancholy and such sicknesses and afflictions as rheumatism. It is also used as a fever cure, at which time it is placed in a yellow cloth and tied about the neck, but once the fever is cured, the stone must be discarded.

CHEOPS—A king of Egypt, approx. 2,900 B.C. The builder of the Great Pyramid near Gizeh, he was well versed in the occult and reportedly did a masterful job in including various mystical and religious approaches in the contruction of the Pyramid.

CHIROMANCY—A form of astral physiognomy, q.v., which involves divination from the palm of the hand. The lines and seven mounts of the palm are analyzed for dominant relationships and characteristics. The mounts are small protuberances at the base of the fingers and thumb, and the degree of the development of each influences the characteristics of the individual. The lines and mounts are related to and named after planets, which, in turn, have the names and characteristics of Greek and Roman gods. Thus, an individual with a well-developed mount of Jupiter—at the base of the index finger—is "read" as having plentiful quantities of the characteristics of ambition, honor, felicity, and religion. The lines are not given an astral connection, rather they are called heart, life, head, and fortune lines, depending on the deepness and length of each for representative traits.

CIRCE—A Greek enchantress who had the power to turn men into swine. See TRANSFORMATIONS.

CLAIRAUDIENCE—The faculty for hearing spiritual sounds which are not hallucinatory in nature and which may or may not be heard by other persons but which have a supernatural origin. Many clairaudients hear messages in which a prophecy or other information is given. There have been claims made by musicians and poets that they have heard passages of music or poetry which they later published but ascribed to a supernatural agency. This is highly speculative and, unless there is some concrete revelation presented, open to suspicion as delusional or of the individual's own creation.

A good example of clairaudience is that of Joan of Arc, but she was not the only religious figure who claimed to hear voices.

Through recent standards of definitions, the term has come to require some prophecy or information from which the reception may be verified as originating from an external source.

CLAIRVOYANCE—A supernatural ability to see events, persons, and things which are remote in time and location, and of which no knowledge can reach the seer by any sensory channel considered normal. It is an agency which involves the use of senses in a manner not explained in terms of any scientific information now available.

Clairvoyance may include premonitions of events which will take place in the future, of events which have taken place in the past but of which the seer could not possibly have knowledge, and of events currently taking place at a great distance.

The term is also used to include the power to see spirit bodies, but since this is covered in such terms as mediumship, apparitions, astral bodies, etc., this reference has gradually fallen from current use.

Descriptions of clairvoyance in relation to premonitions generally describe the seer as witnessing an event or persons as they perform various activities, but there are reports of clairvoyant precognition in which the seer is shown documents or handwriting which tell of forthcoming events. See also PRECOGNITION, PREMONITION, PROPHETS.

CLAN—A social structure, usually familial in primitive societies, and banded together for some purpose or under some mystic or religious sign, which is a totem, q.v. Clans will often adopt some animal or bird as its chief totem and ascribe miraculous, magical powers to it. Many clans have rites of healing, magic, and curses. They will carefully initiate new members into the use of appropriate charms and the wearing of amulets, talismans, or other good-luck features. By combining spiritual powers, they may entreat or cause gods and spirits to perform favors for them.

CLIO—In Greek mythology, one of the nine muses, q.v., representing history.

COHOBA—A semi-ritual hallucinogenic drug found in the West Indies, Northern and Central South America. The pods and seeds of the plant are dried, ground into a powder, and inhaled through a Y-shaped tube. The effects are strange visions, temporary madness, wild excitement, and then a long period of tranquility. The user often has visions of prophecy in connection with himself as an individual or member of a clan, or in relationship to being remiss in his duties to one or more spirits.

COMBUST—An astrological term denoting a condition in which a given planet moves closer than five degrees toward the sun.

CONCEPT THERAPY—A method of healing and mobilizing with thought originated by Dr. Thurmond Fleet, an American chiropractor. Although there are some superficial comparisons to be made with Christian Science, Concept Therapy is less concerned with the nature of matter and the mind over matter doctrine than it is with the mobilization of internal forces. Highly modernized in technique and well aware of many modern psychological approaches, Concept Therapy has as one of its slogans, "Heal with ideas." See *Psychic Self-Improvement for the Millions* by William Wolff, for detailed discussions of Dr. Fleet, the Concept Therapy Institute and the entire movement.

CONSCIOUSNESS EXPANDERS—Powerful drugs which seem to give greater abilities of concentration. See PSYCHEDELICS.

CORAL—A hard substance composed of the skeletons of sea life. Used as a protective amulet against plague and pestilence. It reportedly loses its color when a friend of the wearer is about to die.

CONTAGIOUS MAGIC—An off-shoot of sympathetic magic, q.v., in which it is believed that things once joined must remain forever joined, at least in theory. And things severed will attempt to rejoin and, at the very least, offer a positive attraction. Thus, a piece of rock is said to seek reunion with the larger rock from which it was chipped.

On a more personal level, bits of hair, nails, skin, and bones, once removed from an individual may be used against him in such ritual magics as voodoo. The belief is that whatever is done to the scrap of hair, skin nail, etc., will also befall the individual.

Throughout Europe, there is a widespread belief that the umbilical cord of the individual must be carefully preserved, particularly against immersion in water or fire, lest the person to whom it was once attached die by drowning or fire.

Some Pacific and Asiatic people believe that any significant part of the body, fingers, toes, limbs, etc. lost during life must be reunited with the physical body before the spirit can move on to the next world.

CONJURE—To practice either black or white magic; to summon a demon, spirit, etc. by oath, magic spell, or incantation.

COSMOGONY—Mystic divination by the type of weather in a given day.

COVEN—A meeting of witches and demons, in which the Black Mass is often recited and sacrilegious anthems sung. Sexual orgies are common and victims are brought in to be slaughtered, eaten, bewitched, and tortured.

CROOKES, SIR WILLIAM—A noted English scientist, inventor, and psychical researcher who literally put his reputation as a scientist and member of the Royal Academy on the chopping block because of his interest and belief in the world of psychic phenomena. He is noted for his researches into the alleged seances and levitations performed by another noted English psychic, Daniel Dunglas Home. But his most famous association was with the medium, Florence Cook, allegedly the first spiritualist to present the phenomenon of complete materialization. Miss Cook's spiritual control was Katie King, allegedly the daughter of a pirate. The seances at which Sir William was an observer and commentator caused such publicity that a scandal arose involving him and Miss Cook. The reputations of both suffered, although Sir

William's attempts at gaining concrete proof of Miss Cook's materializations seem admirable. As late as 1965, the entire Crookes-Cook scandal was reopened by an English journalist, who leveled charges of duplicity and conspiracy at Sir William, alleging that the scientist had been taken in by the spiritualist and that he had become her lover. A well-documented defense was presented by an American journalist, James Crenshaw, who alleged that the charges of fraud against Sir William were all circumstantial. In any case, nearly every detailed source on psychic research, particularly in the field of seances and materializations, contains entries on Sir William, who was probably one of the most scrupulous researchers of his day.

CROSS—Generally a figure with four arms, mounted at varying degrees or attitudes ranging from the T, or tau cross, to the X, or cross of St. Andrew, and the familiar Christian cross. Probably descended from various hieroglyphics and religious signs such as the swastika and ankh, both of which see. Each cross had some special importance or representation; common among these meanings were life, power, mystical ability, strength, eternal life, etc. The Christian cross became, in time, an actual symbol of Christ and was used as a religious medal and as an amulet by mystics. Few religious or mystical philosophies are lacking a symbol with some form of cross.

CROWLEY ALEISTAR—An English spiritualist and diabolist who specialized in forming magical cults for the study of the occult. There was no doubting his sincerity, but many critics have doubted his sanity. Evolving many theories based on combinations of Rosecrucianism, Eastern religions, and occult philosophies, he took to the use of drugs to induce ecstasies and had many followers with whom he engaged in bizarre sexual orgies and excesses. One of Crowley's beliefs was that the orgasm provided a mystical communication with the forces of magic and occult. Each orgasm brought the individual closer to an understanding of that power.

He started several retreats, the most famous of which was located in Sicily.

CUARNADERO—A Mexican witch doctor or medicine man. Although he is able to work some evil and has a reputation for this capacity, he is best known as a medicine man who effects cures and beneficial spells and assists in appeasing the gods. In communities where such hallucinogenic agents as peyote or the sacred mushroom are used for religious purposes, he presides over the opening ceremonies. Some degree of folk medicine cures have been attributed to him, and in some cases, he is spoken of as a faith healer or one who cures by a laying on of hands.

CULMINATION—In astrology, the arrival of a planet at a point known as midheaven, the cusp of the tenth house.

CURES—In addition to magical and related remedies to be discussed throughout this dictionary, following are some remedies in common practice with clear-cut beliefs shown in magical, supernatural, and occult methods:

The touch of a dead man's hand as a cure of eczema; toothache ceases when the gum is rubbed with a dead finger; the dust from a new grave cures consumption; the cat cure—having a sickly child drink milk from a milk bottle and then having a cat finish the milk so that the disease would be transferred to the animal.

CURSE—An adverse incantation directing the wrath and other possible consequences from God, spirits, demons, devils, etc. to a specific person or group of persons to accomplish a nefarious purpose.

CUSP—In astrology, an imaginary line used to separate a house of the zodiac from either of its two immediate neighbors. Thus, Sagittarius would be separated from each of its immediate neighbors, Scorpio and Capricorn, by cusps. An individual is considered to be born on the cusp of two signs when his birth occurs at a time when the sun is moving from one house to another. Being born on the cusp of two houses would give an individual characteristics of both signs.

D

DAIMON—An ancient concept of a spiritual guardian or angel assigned to each soul.

DANCE OF THE WITCH DOCTOR—Preparatory to a vision or state of ecstasy, the native witch doctor begins a dance which is strictly governed by the number of steps in each movement. The dance begins slowly and increases in tempo, usually ending when he falls to the ground, exhausted. The words he utters then are said to be blessed. Many witch doctors, particularly in Africa, will move in the set pattern of steps for as long as twelve or sixteen hours before falling, and even so, the elaborate formulas for interpreting the divine or mystic meanings of their utterances are so filled with loopholes that the entire project may have to be repeated.

DAYS, EPAGOMENAL OR INTERCALARY—The five days added to the calendar, increasing it from 360 to 365 days per year. A special god was assigned to each of these days, and the arrival of Osiris was said to have occurred on the first of the five epagomenal days.

DEATH, ABILITY TO FORETELL—A special gift of precognition or divination many sensitives are born with. Usually the predictions come in dreams, but some sensitives have visions and a few suddenly have intuitive flashes. In either case, these adepts know who is going to die, when, where, and how. They do not necessarily have to know the victim personally.

DEATH, EARLY OF SENSITIVES—A belief that close intimacy with the spirit world weakens the vital powers of a mortal and causes death at an early age. This belief has come under great attack during the past century, when the life span of nearly all persons, sensitives and nonsensitives alike, has been increased. The probable origin of the belief is from ancient or medieval times, when it was believed that a spiritual adept was the target of jealousy spells from witches, sorcerers, etc.

DEMONS—Evil spirits. Christians believe them to be servants of the devil, but many persons believe they are the souls of evil men who once walked the earth and elected to serve the dark forces. Demons may be propitiated by gifts or controlled by magic spells and charms, but their essentially malevolent natures make them dangerous companions or servants. See also FAMILIAR.

DEMONOLOGY—A branch of black magic which deals with malevolent spirits, cataloging these beings according to their powers, the degree of evil they possess, and any special abilities they might contain. Demonology also records the spells and charms needed to keep demons subservient, making it an extremely valuable study for any person who wishes strong supernatural powers of evil.

DENTALIA—Sea shells of a particular nature found along the California and Oregon coastlines and used as cutting edges and ornaments by the coastal Indians, but as money by Indians farther inland. The Indians who used dentalia as money did so in the belief that the scarcity of these mussel shells to them made their use as money a practical matter. Having dentalia and using it as an object on which to concentrate supposedly caused more shells to come to the owner. By the same token, using the dentalia as an agent to concentrate on women could cause the owner to have more wives offered to him.

DESTINY—Often used synonymously with fate or luck.

That which is to be. The sum total of experiences and activities to come. Occultists, whether astrologers, palmists, spiritualists, etc., are divided in their opinions of whether or not destiny may be bent to the will of the individual; those who believe destiny is inflexible are often called fatalists. But all agree that destiny may be discovered before it has been fulfilled. Often linked with karma, q.v.

DESTROYING ANGEL—popular name for amanita phalloides, a beautiful fungus which grows in "fairy rings" and which may cause intense hallucinations and/or death.

DEVIL—The Satanic majesty. The Prince of Darkness. A powerful deity of evil, often interpreted as being Lucifer, the fallen angel. The ubiquity of this concept is as great as the concept of God. In Christianity and Judaism, there is one supreme ruler of evil who is the arch foe of the forces of goodness, headed by God. Like God, the Devil is immortal and indestructible. Demons may be bribed or captured by magic; the Devil is implacable. The Egyptian god Set is the counterpart of the Christian concept of the Devil. He personifies physical darkness and moral wickedness. He waged war against the Sun god, Her-ur and was defeated but not slain. Set was the foe of men and none could escape him except with the intervention of Osiris who, like Christ, suffered human birth and death. Occasionally, as in the Book of Job, the Devil is conceived to be a colleague or servant of God.

DHARMA-KAYA—The state of perfect enlightenment in which the soul perceives a dazzling bright light, the primordial light or pure knowledge which signifies a joining or union.

DIAKKA—Astral bodies which, on the death of the physical body, are destined for immediate periods of education before being allowed to enjoy the potential for future advancement. The name is usually given to spirits which were, during mortality, ignorant, underdeveloped, or malevolent, but for whom there is hope of redemption. Supposedly, the spirits retain these very characteristics for a time in the astral world and learn to progress beyond them from contact with more highly developed spirits.

DIAMOND—This gem, when tied to the left arm of the wearer, becomes an amulet of invincibility. It is also a protection against enchantments and, in some countries, is believed to be able to counter the effects of magnetism.

DIANA—The Roman goddess of the moon, wild animals, and the hunt. She is often identified with the Greek goddess Artemis, who is an exact counterpart. Both frequently appeared on earth at the full moon, in the shape of a deer.

DIANETICS—A modern eclectic philosophy with some occult overtones. See SCIENTOLOGY and HUBBARD, L. RON

DIONYSUS—The Greek god of vegetation, wine, and drunkenness. A counterpart of Bacchus, q.v., and very fond of revelry. He will often preside over the agape or love feast.

DIRECT WRITING—As opposed to automatic writing; this is direct written communication from the spirit world without the use of a physical medium or agent. Often, a mischievous spirit or poltergeist will complete an unfinished letter which has been left unattended or, in more modern times, leave messages on a piece of paper left in an unattended typewriter. It is employed as a means of communication by both good-intentioned and malevolent spirits. It is performed without any assistance from mortals and would thus exclude messages received on an ouija board unless the planchette or marking device moved over the board without any mortal hands placed on it. Another favorite location for a direct writing message is a blackboard.

DISEASES CAUSED BY SPIRITS—A wide-spread belief throughout the world, still prevalent. Some say the spirits single out a victim and deliberately infect him, either in mischief or in hopes of an offering. Others hold that an angry spirit takes possession of the victim and, by its very presence, causes disease-like symptoms or possible madness. Generally speaking, spirits which cause diseases are pacified with offerings, prayers, and charms, but the spirits which possess are more stubborn and require various forms of exorcism involving loud noises, shock, sudden immersion in cold water, and other physical punishments. If the victim should die during this exorcism, it is usually said that the spirit would not have let loose under any circumstances and that death was the only release.

DIVINATION—Any method of obtaining knowledge, either of the future or past and contemporary events, not available through any normal source. Such branches of the occult as phrenology, astrology, chiromancy, tea leaf reading, pedomancy, etc. are all matters of divination. In derivation, the term means a message from a god or supernatural agency which may be made available to man provided certain requirements are met. These requirements generally involve a form of sanctification and ritual purification or knowledge unavailable to most humans. References to divination are scattered through this book. They include poison oracles, divination through the use of hallucinogenics, and the reading of the future from such varied sources as eggs, palms of hands, human and animal entrails, crystal balls, etc. Closely related to prophecy and oracles, both of which see. It may also occur involuntarily to anyone, whether an occult adept or not, and there is no guarantee that the information received will be beneficial to the seer.

DIVINERS—Includes sorcerers, fortune tellers, shamans, etc., all of whom will be found throughout the book. In general, any mortal adept in the art of interpreting supernatural messages presented through one or more agencies.

DIVINE PLANT OF THE INCAS—Coca; the plant which is the only known source of cocaine. Coca leaves have been chewed by Peruvian natives since the time of the Incas, supposedly to give them the endurance of the gods.

DIXON, JEANNE—(1913-   ) American author, prophet, and psychical adept who has been widely consulted as a source by noted personalities, all of whom attest to the great accuracy of her predictions, which apparently come from a supernormal source.

DJINN—Born of fire, they may appear to humans in the form of monsters, serpents, cats, and even human beings. They may become invisible, but there is an ointment which humans may put on their eyes which will enable them to see djinns at any time. Good djinns are attractive in appearance; evil djinns are quite ugly in appearance and sometimes compel men to serve them as slaves.

DOLLS—The use of dolls in magic or worship is world-wide. Incantations and other rituals bring the doll to life. In some instances, the burning of a charm written in blood is used. The life force of the doll is a spirit or part of a spirit which has been placed in it by magic. The spirit or part of the spirit of a man which may be placed in a doll is some intimate part of his body such as spittle, hair, nail parings, etc. Then, whatever is done to the doll happens to the man, as per descriptions in contagious or sympathetic magics, both of which see.

DONKEY TEETH—Often used as amulets or parts of medicine bags, they were considered tokens of good fortune.

DOOR FOR SPIRITS—As the Irish were in the habit of placing a pipe on the door stoop for the "little people" to smoke and the Scots were accustomed to leaving bowls of cream for the brownies, many African tribes were in the habit of placing a special small door in their huts. This door is reserved for use by the spirits of their ancestors, who supposedly live with their mortal relatives and who are always at hand to help.

DOPPLEGANGER—Often referred to as a double; a ghost which greatly resembles a living person. In some cases, the ghost not only looks like its human counterpart but also resembles him in speech. Doubles have been seen by the persons they mirror as well as by others. Like most ghosts, in spite of the near-perfect imitation of life, the double often floats above the ground. German origin.

DOWSING—The practice by which one is supposed to find underground supplies of water, either by means of a divining rod or with "feelings" in the hands. It is known as divining, water witching, and rhabdomancy. If an indicator other than bare hands is used, it is variously called a divining rod, dowsing rod, witching stick, dipping rod, striking stick, or wand. Currently, the word dowsing is finding the most use. A reference in the Old Testament (Numbers) to Moses, striking a rock with his rod and thus producing water for his followers has caused enthusiasts of water witching to believe it a god-given talent. Marco Polo reported the use of the divining rod in the Orient and Herodotus mentions its use by the Persians, Scythians, and Medes.

The most common witching stick is a Y-shaped green twig cut from a hazel, willow, or peach tree. The two forks vary from 14 to 18 inches in length and the neck from 4 to 11 inches. The diameter of the stick is generally not more than an inch. There are some records of aluminum rods and, in various parts of the U.S., branches of apple, dogwood, pinon, juniper, and maple trees are used.

The usual technique of employing the divining rod is the grasping of the two branches of the forked twig, one in each hand, with the bottom of the Y pointed skyward. The dowser then walks over the ground in an area where a supply of water is desired. When he walks over an underground supply of water, the dowsing stick is supposed to dip down, pointing directly to a water supply. A stake is driven into the spot and the digging of a well is begun.

Some dowsers claim to be able to predict the exact depth at which the water will be found. Others claim only the ability to locate the water supply.

One explanation for the principle of water witching is based on contagious magic; the moisture in the green twig is attracted to the underground source. Another theory is that the stick is an antenna for electrical currents which run through the body of the dowser. According to custom, water witches are born, not developed.

At one time, it was believed that only the most simpleminded could function successfully as a dowser, but subsequently, men with advanced degrees in engineering and the sciences have shown an amazingly high percentage of "hits" in dowsing.

DOWSER—A water witch. One who locates hidden or underground water supplies.

DRAGON—A large, reptilian monster, often with more than one head. Able to belch smoke and vomit fire, the monster often guarded treasures, enchanted castles, or areas of magical significance.

DREAMS—Pictures and impressions experienced in a sleeping, trance, or drugged state. Not only do dreams foretell the future, they may be used as a special meeting place for the spirits of the dead and the gods to communicate with humans. Often these dreams are presented in symbol, requiring an interpretation of them by a shaman, medicine man, etc. Of special significance to primitive tribes, where certain magical dreams determine the future and possible clan or moiety membership of the individual. See MEDICINE DREAMS.

DREAM SOUL—The part of a man's spirit which leaves him during sleep, supposedly to adventure away from the physical body. If the dream soul does not return before the man awakens, he may sicken and die unless a witch doctor can coax the two elements back together. Note similarity to astral body, q.v.

DRUIDS—A highly mystical and magical race, nearly all of them adept in the magical arts. With a homeland in what is now England, the Druids were responsible for many of the incantations and spells which control the elements, appease the gods, and insure the growing of crops. They supposedly controlled abilities of invisibility, transmutation, spells, and charms. They were also versed in astrology and other forms of magic. Their domain also included France and Ireland and they were particularly influential before the Celtic peoples—whom they influenced the most—became Christianized. As a group, they represent one of the highest orders of magical adepts, ranking with the Mayans and Incas.

DUKUN—A Malay practitioner and shaman who sells charms and spells.

DYBBUK—One of the greatest fears and superstitions found among the East European Jews of the Middle Ages; a belief in spirit possession by which the physical body of a man or woman could become the host for a demon who was so powerful that it could exercise complete control over its host. The will and personality of an individual so possessed were extinguished and could be restored only by the most powerful exorcisms. The dybbuk particularly delighted in fastening itself to the soul of a scholar. In more current use, among Jews and non-Jews, the term has come to mean a restless spirit who has sinned so greatly in a past life that it has been denied peace for some time and is desperately seeking some identity.

E

EARTH, DIVINATION BY—Use of earth formations, dirt or sand patterns to divine. See GEOMANCY.

EARTH MOTHER—Certain powerful goddesses who embodied the manifestation of the female principle were said to have taken a special endowing care of earth. Among these are Ishtar, Erda, Freya, Hel, Kali, and Demeter. Each was worshipped as though she had direct influence over the creation of Earth.

EARTH SPIRITS—Supernatural beings which may assist humans. See FAIRIES.

EBONY—A wood possessing strong innate magical powers. Magicians used it for their wands and other ritualistic paraphernalia.

ECTENIC FORCE—A supernatural force which emanates from a medium and may be directed by him to move physical objects. In some spiritualistic circles, it is believed that spirits who are unable to materialize will provide the medium with ectenic force in order to move apports. Also closely related with psychokinesis and levitation, both of which see, the term has fallen from use because of its apparent ambiguity.

ECTOPLASM—A vaporous, luminescent substance supposed to emanate from the body of the medium during a trance. This substance is spiritual in origin and is offered as proof of the spiritual world and of the power of the medium. Ectoplasm is also supposed to be the composition of spiritual manifestations in the form of human beings.

EDDY, MARY BAKER—(1821–1910) An American religious leader and founder of the Christian Science movement.

EIGHT—The number of regeneration. Most old baptistries are octagonal in shape. The Old Testament specifies that the male child shall be circumcised on the eighth day of his life. In Egypt, the company of Thoth contained eight deities. An American publisher of occult books and pamphlets, Orson Fowler, maintained than an octagonal house was the most conducive to good health.

EIGHTH HOUSE, THE—In astrology, the house of death. See ZODIAC, HOUSES OF.

EL DORADO—The king of the Golden City on the Amazon River, said to have been discovered by early explorers. The king wore gold dust on his garments as a charm and an amulet against death, sickness, and attack, hence his name, El Dorado, the one covered with gold, or the gold one.

ELECTRIC GIRLS, THE—Young girls in their early teens who allegedly caused various psychic phenomena such as the moving of objects at a distance, the levitation of tables, chairs, brooms, small animals, etc. There is a distinct relationship between the abilities of these girls and the presence of poltergeists, q.v., when young girls are in the area.

ELEMENTS—The four basic elements are earth, air, fire, and water. Virgo, Capricorn, and Taurus are the zodiacal signs for earth and are called earth signs; Gemini and Aquarius are air signs; Aries, Leo and Sagittarius are Fire signs; and Pisces, Scorpio, and Cancer are water signs.

ELEVEN—While not a mystic number, it is considered a bad omen for the person who dreams of it.

ELEVENTH HOUSE, THE—In astrology, the house of friends. See ZODIAC, HOUSES OF.

ELF—A Scandinavian fairy. They are supernatural beings who delight in mischief, particularly the bands of Black elves who cause sickness and injury. These live underground and are ruled by an extraordinarily ugly elf king.

In Ireland, the Black elves are said to sicken cattle by shooting small arrows into them.

The Danes believe the elves were rebel angels who were cast out of heaven. Others believe they sprang from the children of Adam and Lilith.

ELIXER OF LIFE, THE—Usually a fluid although sometimes a powder, this supernatural potion could extend life and heal fatal wounds over an indefinite period. Nearly all magical backgrounds have such an elixir or potion. In some cases, it is awarded for the performance of deeds, in other cases, it is found after a search similar to the search for the Holy Grail.

EMBALMING—In order to achieve eternal life, the Egyptians believed the body must be kept intact. At first, they preserved bodies by baking them in the sun or with the help of a small fire. Later, the more familiar art of embalming with spices, honey, and sweet-smelling ingredients developed. A part of the embalming ritual, according to the Egyptians, states that a mummy will be visited by gods to be assured of everlasting life.

EMBRACE—Power or vital energy may be transferred in an embrace. The embrace may be used for good or evil purposes and great souls or holy persons will give some of their spiritual power in such a manner. However, an evil being may take power from an unsuspecting victim while embracing him and, thus, gain control. The laying on of hands, q.v., had its origin in the practice of the power-giving embrace.

EMERALD—A precious stone used as an amulet to protect the wearer from the evil eye, epileptic seizures, and fascination with evil things.

EMETICS—A chemically induced vomiting agent and

standard item in the pharmacology of the witch doctor. It is used in cases where the patient is possessed by an evil spirit; it is hoped that the patient will vomit out the evil spirit or will have spasms of such intensity as to cause the spirit discomfort enough to cause it to leave of its own accord.

Occasionally, emetics are used to determine guilt in an ordeal. The suspect is forced to swallow the emetic. If it produces nausea and causes him to vomit easily, he is innocent; if it causes vertigo and causes him to lose self-control, he is assumed guilty of the charge against him.

ENLIGHTENMENT—Knowledge or experience of God. It cannot be achieved by will or force; it is the ultimate goal of spiritual development.

ENTRAILS—The inner organs of animals used in divination. In different parts of the world, different animals are used as a source. The use of chickens, sheep, and goats is quite common. See also DIVINATION.

ENVOÛTEMENT—The magical practice of making a figurine of wax, then abusing it with needles, pins, flames, etc., so that the designated human victim will suffer similar pains, indignities or even death. Special spells and incantations must be chanted by the magician as he tortures the wax figurine. Especially associated with voodoo rites. See also CONTAGIOUS MAGIC.

ENVY—The source of the evil eye. Even if the lips of the envious man give praise, he can make a magical mental reservation while he looks at his victim, causing the exact opposite of his words to take place. Envy and jealousy are strongly linked to the evil eye, and become repositories for evil spirits or at least the means by which evil spirits may enter the body.

EPAGOMENAL GODS—Osiris, Isis, Typhon, Apollo, and Aphrodite. See DAYS, EPAGOMENAL.

EPILEPSY—Once believed to be caused by possession. The Greeks thought this possession was a benevolent spirit; the Jews and Christians believed it was caused by a diabolic possession.

ERATO—One of the nine muses, q.v., she was the patron of love poetry.

E.S.P.—Extrasensory perception, the ability to experience beyond the normal range of the senses. Used to generalize all the possible experiences which may befall man and for which there is no apparent explanation. Thus, a spiritualistic medium has certain E.S.P. abilities as does the sender and recipient of telepathic communications. See also PSI ABILITIES.

ESPANTO—Magic fright which does not affect the soul nor provide serious psychological consequences.

ETERNITY—A concept beyond words. Illimitable time in the past and beyond.

It is regarded as everlasting time which is the property of a personal god, or of a state which is beyond all concept of time. It is an attribute of an all-encompassing godhead and is related to infinity.

EUTERPE—In Greek mythology, the muse of music and lyric poetry. See MUSES.

EVIL—Its existence has never been satisfactorily explained, but nevertheless, its presence is as old as man and it is generally regarded as a force which is in constant opposition with God and god-fearing man. The Hindus believe evil is an attribute of God, but to be defined by man. The Christians, Jews, and Mohammedans believe it is defined by God. No religion believes evil may be destroyed per se, but many speak of a time when most evil will disappear from the world.

EVIL EYE—Strong but wicked persons—sometimes in league with the devil—have the ability to curse with a look. Belief is worldwide. Its effect may be vitiated or prevented by a preventative amulet or the burning of proper charms. Especially dangerous to children and pregnant women, some occultists say it is a specific part of the mind, focusing its power through the organ of the eye. In some European countries, belief in the evil eye is so strong that persons suspected of possessing it are blinded or murdered in their sleep.

EXORCISM—A casting out of evil spirits by means of ritual, incantation, charm, incense, magic, gift, bribe, or counter-spell, or by any combination of these. It is used to remove a demon or evil spirit from the physical host it may inhabit, or it may be used to remove one or more spirits from a dwelling or other gathering place. It always signifies some occupancy of some person or place by an undesirable spirit who is to be removed.

In some cases, the exorcism becomes so violent that the human being who is possessed will die, but this is still considered a victory since the spirit is now trapped in the physical body while the soul of the departed may move on to a more congenial spiritual atmosphere.

F

FAIRIES—Generally English, Scottish, and Irish in origin, they are benevolent little people who help mortals with their work, bring gifts, and preserve an atmosphere of happiness. They are often called The Wee Folk or The Little People and are attractive in appearance as opposed to brownies, q.v., If they are angered, the fairies will not hesitate to punish. They have been known to kidnap children.

In Scandinavian countries, the fairies are called The White Elves. They are supernatural, immortal, and usually invisible. Their size varies from that of a young child to normal adult size. Some say the fairies are fallen angels, others believe they are the souls of departed men and women, still others think of them as earth-bound spirits who are working off cosmic debts.

FAITH—An inner conviction supported by some evidence or tenet of belief. An essential part of most forms of worship; although it is also required for the black arts. Faith in the occult forces is supposed to ensure the believer a spiritual protector with powers in direct proportion to the believer's own faith, this in the case of encounter with evil spirits.

FAITH HEALING—Curing illness through mental and emotional means and generally without the use of herbs, instruments, or utensils. In some cases of faith healing, the patient must have faith that he will be cured, in other cases, he is supposedly cured on the strength of the abilities of the practitioner, and in yet other cases, both patient and practitioner must display evidences of faith, giving each an out if the cure fails.

Some American Indians deliberately provoke painful prerituals as a preparation for the healing. Depending on his reaction to this pain, the healer may determine if his ministrations will be beneficial.

Some faith healers are devoutly religious, believing their power to heal comes from a divine source. Incidents are reported in Africa, South America, and the Philippines of such healers actually performing complex surgery without instruments or anesthetics. See PSYCHIC SURGEONS.

The laying on of hands, q.v., is a type of healing by faith. Some healers, such as Christian Science practitioners, do not need to touch their patient and indeed may even perform their feats at a great distance from the patient.

A modern American type of healing, related more

specifically to psychic disturbances and disorders is White Magic Group Therapy, q.v.

FAITH HEALERS, FAMOUS—Cagliostro treated European nobility by mysticism and alchemy during the time of Louis XVI.

James Graham opened the Temple of Health in England, employed certain of Cagliostro's cures and invented a bed which insured conception.

Andrea Jackson Davis, an American healer, wrote a popular book of instruction on the metaphysics of health.

The Earl of Sandwich was a layer on of hands.

Kathryn Kuhlman, a contemporary American faith healer, is a layer on of hands to achieve cures of sickness and lameness.

FALLING SICKNESS, THE—Sudden seizures which supposedly marked a person favored by the gods. Julius Caesar was thusly afflicted. SEE EPILEPSY.

FAMILIAR—The spirit companion of a witch; it follows her bidding and may take the shape of a cat, insect, or dog. Some familiars have been known to get a witch with child. The offspring of such a union is always a monster. By the use of incantations, some mortals may secure the services of a familiar.

FASCINUM—An amulet in the form of a phallus, worn—especially by children—as a protection against the evil eye.

FASTS—Periods during which the worshipper or magician abstains from food and often from water as well. Fasts are frequently used to bring important visions of divination. SEE MEDICINE DREAM—In some religions, fasts are used as a penance, in others, they are employed to evoke pity from the gods. Fasts are also believed to have healing qualities.

FAT, HUMAN—Often used an an unguent by witches in

black magic rituals; occasionally offered as a sacrilegious sacrament in the black mass.

FATES, THE THREE—Clotho, the spinner; Lachesis, the disposer of lots; and Atropos, the Unchangeable, who cuts the thread of life.

FATICARIA—A name given in some Latin countries to a witch, q.v.

FÂTIHAT—A greatly venerated Muslim prayer, found at the beginning of the Koran. Like the sign of the cross, it protects against evil and particularly against witchcraft. It is often reproduced on a slip of paper and carried as an amulet.

FAUST, JOHANN—A sixteenth century German magician and astrologer who is believed by the ignorant to have sold his soul to the Devil for the gift of occult knowledge, power, and youth.

FAYRUZ—The lucky stone. SEE TURQUOISE.

FEÉ—A French origin fairy which lived in Normandy and acted as a toll keeper for bridges. Humans were made to dance for a safe crossing. If they refused the fee, they would be seized and hurled off the bridge, into the water. Possible origin of the word "fee," for payment. Also called *Les Dames Blanches*, the white ladies.

FELDSPAR—A hard green stone which, when worn as an amulet, protected the wearer against sunstroke and headache.

FERTILITY RITES—Sometimes called orgies; the formal intercourse of a priest with a selected virgin or of a priest and priestess, or a priestess with a king, or all the men in a village. Held for the purpose of encouraging the crops and general bounty of nature. A very ancient ritual, portions of which were traced to the Druids.

FETISH—An object made by humans to protect against evil, to heal the sick, or to secure the user a desired effect, such as potency, fertility, love, etc. A simple fetish is made from a substance which has magical powers. A complex or "artificial" fetish has a powerful medicine like the gall bladder of a crocodile or the urine of a virgin added to it. The complex fetish is usually quite detailed and may resemble a doll with humanoid or god-like features.

FIFTEEN—A sacred number in the Kabbalah, q.v. It has the numerical value of YH, one of the names of God, and its use is as powerful as the use of the name of God.

FIFTH HOUSE—In astrology, the house of parents and their influence. See ZODIAC, SIGNS OF.

FIFTY—The number of the Holy Spirit. The Law was dictated to Moses on Mt. Sinai on the fiftieth day following Israel's departure from Egypt.

FIGURES, PROPHYLACTIC—Fetishes in the shape of human figures which have the ability to ward off evil because of their posture and because of the incantations which are chanted while handling them.

FINGER AMULETS—Amulets made of human fingers, usually the little finger of the right hand. Considered one of the most powerful forms of protection against evil; an attraction for the strong, benevolent occult powers.

FINGERS—In palmistry, an astrological planet rules each part of the hand; Venus the thumb, Mars the palm, Moon the heel, Jupiter the first finger, Saturn the second, Sun the third, and Mercury the fourth.

FIRE—One of the four mystical elements. See ELEMENTS.

FISH—A symbol of Jesus Christ, because of the Greek word for fish, *icthyos*, being an acronym for Jesus Christ, Son of God, the Savior. As a result, figures of fish were often used as amulets by early Christians.

FISHES—In astrology, a sign of the zodiac, symbolized by a fish. See PISCES; ZODIAC, SIGNS OF.

FIVE—Symbolic of completeness, five is considered a

lucky number. Solomon's seal was five pointed. Christ suffered five wounds which are called The Well of Pity, The Well of Mercy, The Well of Grace, the Well of Comfort, and The Well of Everlasting Life.

FLAGELLUM DAEMONUM—A famous occult source book by Mengus, listing cures for those individuals possessed by the Devil. Among the remedies are salt, wine, water, incense, gold, and honey. The book also contains recipes of countermagic to be used against spellcasters.

FLUID OF LIFE, THE—Another name for a magical, life and youth sustaining fluid. See ELIXIR OF LIFE.

FORT, CHARLES—(1874–1932) American author, newspaperman, occultist, whose most important works were a series of compilations of occult and supernatural incidents for which there were no normal explanations. His most important work, *The Book of the Damned*, made his reputation. *New Land, Lo!* and *Wild Talents* convinced his many readers and followers that he had direct access to the spiritual world and could cause supernormal phenomena.

FORTUNE, LINE OF—In palmistry, a line on the human hand which may be interpreted by length, depth, etc. See LINES.

FORTUNE TELLER—Usually a diviner or palmist or astrologer, often a reader of tealeaves. A medium of psychic sensitivity with some powers of divination. Some astrologers violently resent being called fortune tellers, since the terms has fallen into disrepute and connotes quackery. See DIVINATION, DIVINERS.

FOURTH HOUSE—In astrology, the house of children. See ZODIAC, HOUSES OF.

FOX, KATIE, and MARGARETTA—Believed to be the first spiritualistic mediums in the United States. In 1848, a series of rappings were heard at the Fox household and, through a series of questions, it was discovered that the rappings were probably responses from some intelligent being, allegedly spiritual. Further questionings elicited the story of a murder, performed on a former occupant of the house. Following instructions from the spirits, the two young girls allegedly found human remains in the cellar. They were taken to psychic researchers by their parents and attempts were made to discredit them. But wherever the two girls went, rappings followed them. Subsequent charges of possible fraud failed to stem the enormous tide of interest in spiritualism in America begun by the two young girls. The fact of their sex and youth has caused many psychic researchers to believe that they attracted poltergeists, q.v.

FOX TAIL—The tail of the fox was used as an amulet to protect domestic animals from the evil eye. This later included mechanical vehicles. Note modern custom of attaching fox tails to automobiles.

FRAU BERT—A female devil; not a witch but a metaphysical being.

FRAZER, SIR JAMES—Author of *The Golden Bough,* which outlines ancient and modern magical and religious practices.

FRIDAY NIGHT—Sabbath for witches.

FRINGE—Possesses supernatural powers. The Lord told Moses to order the children of Israel to fringe the borders of their garments. Amulets with fringes or tassels protect from the evil eye and mischievous spirits.

FROG—Associated with fertility and fecundity. Amulets in the shape of frogs were worn in order to help a woman conceive. For the same reason, women in Central Africa eat frogs.

Because of their association with new life in the Coptic beliefs, they were also used to symbolize resurrection.

JOHN FRUM MOVEMENT, THE—In 1940, a native of the

island of Tanna declared himself the prophet of John Frum, a spirit which replaced an ancient spirit of formerly great power in this South Pacific Island. In his declaration, the prophet said a spirit named John Frum told him the entire island was to change in nature; its volcanic cone would be replaced by fertile plains, its people would be eternally young and healthy and have everything they could possibly desire.

In order to make John Frum's prophecy come true, it was necessary to seek out and kill all Europeans, rid themselves of European customs, and return to the old ways of magic, multiple marriage, ritual drunkenness, etc.

The movement spread through the island, particularly through World War II, and became a part of The Cargo Cult Religion, which spoke of a day of Redemption on which ships filled with cargo would land on the islands, bringing supplies and food for all the faithful.

Interesting comparison with several other religions which have been subverted by Christianity and which, through ritual magic, preach a return to old days and a life of plenty and understanding from the gods. Almost all, in one way or another, wish to rid themselves of European or American influences and return to a worship of their original gods. See also, GHOST DANCE RELIGION.

G

GAFE—The quality some persons have of attracting bad luck and evil. Akin to the evil eye, q.v.

GALL, FRANZ JOSEPH—A Viennese medical philosopher who more or less founded the study of phrenology, q.v., giving his first known lecture on the subject in 1796. He worked on the theory that the human head is, by its shape, an index of the development of the cerebral region beneath, where the location of that particular faculty is located. Gall believed that sufficient research would give him an empirical basis for determining personality traits and disorders through the shape and configuration of the head.

GANESHA—In Hindu religions, the god of wisdom, prudence, and good luck. He is represented as a stout human with the head of an elephant, an animal regarded as quite wise. His own head was lost by an angry glance from a god, but was replaced in its elephantine form by yet other gods. He is represented as having four hands and rides on or is followed by a rat, another animal reputed to be wise.

GANGHA—East Indian word for marihuana or Cannabis sativa.

GARLIC—An amulet against the evil eye, witches, and vampires.

GARNET—As an amulet, this semi-precious stone is used as a protection from evil dreams. It also helps staunch the flow of excessive bleeding from wounds or in menstruation.

GAUFFRIDI—A notorious Satanist who became the spiritual director in an Ursuline Convent in 1610 and caused the nuns who confessed to him to be possessed by the devil.

GAWAIN—In Arthurian legend, one of the most famed and clever of King Arthur's knights; the son of King Lot of Orkney and Morgan Le Fay, Arthur's sister. Well known for his encounter with the Green Knight, whom he smote a tremendous sword blow on the neck. In spite of this seemingly lethal wound, the Green Knight lived and proved to be the most frightening supernatural encounter Gawain had.

CEHENNA—A form of hell in which outrageous tortures were administered but from which the victim could leave on occasion to revisit places known to him during his life. Also held to be a cleansing place preparatory to entering heaven.

GEMINI—In astrology, a sign represented by the twins. See ZODIAC, HOUSES OF.

GEOMANCY—A form of divination based on the special shapes of the earth revealed by random choice. A diviner would drive stakes into the earth as the mood seized him, then connect these with string. The heights, angles, and attitudes formed by the string would influence the divination.

GERONTOCRACY—A form of spiritual and occult ruling by very old men, especially in societies where the young attempt to come into their inheritances at an early age, causing the old to resort to magical arts for protection and status.

GHOST—A visible spirit of a former mortal. Due to the wide and descriptive body of terms available to describe sex, appearance, and purpose, the term has come to be used as a generalization. Used to distinguish between an apparition, which may be the spirit of a dead person, and an astral body.

GHOST-DANCE RELIGION—In American Indian religions, a nationalistic and jingoistic belief which took on a mystical basis. The goal was to force the white man back from whence he came, this in the belief that the buffalo would come again and that there would be no more hunger or deprivation. Manmade and natural elements caused the religion to flourish throughout the West for several years. The killing off of the buffalo, an Indian staple, plus the advent of a series of particularly harsh winters caused Indian shamans and medicine men to consult the spirits. Their divinations told them the spirits, particularly the buffalo spirits, required the death of the White man as a payment for a return to the days of plenty.

In a manner similar to the John Frum Movement in the Pacific, q.v., the spirits not only promised a return to the old ways and the return of the buffalo if their terms were met, they added that life would never be difficult for the faithful again.

As a result, many Plains Indians took up the religion, including the ritual fasts and observances of ritual medicine. They wore white shirts and dressed in buffalo robes for secret rituals.

By 1890, the cult spread through California and into Arizona, where it reached the Navahos with the additional refinement that not only would there be a return to prosperity, the dead would return to life and those who did not believe in the religion would die.

GHOST SICKNESS—In the Navaho Indian, a belief that a ghost or angry spirit may cause an illness which includes as symptoms: fainting, dizziness, bad dreams, sudden feelings of danger, vertigo, confusion, and suffocation. Some are said to have died from this sickness while others have had periods of prolonged fear and loss of appetite and ambition. They believe they are being assaulted by witches or ghosts who are feeding on the ego. A witch doctor is indicated, for countermeasures.

GLOSSALALIA—The speaking in tongues. A verbal adjunct of automatic and direct writing, glossalalia is a means of spirit communication through a human agency, causing the medium to utter words, phrases, and entire, long speeches in foreign languages.

Some mediums have had such experiences, in which they suddenly feel a compulsion to speak, using their own voice. To their bewilderment, the resulting sounds do not apparently make sense. But tape-recorded tongue speakings have revealed that messages were being delivered in languages ranging from Ancient and Modern

Greek through French, Swiss, German, and on down to obscure dialects of primitive tribes.

Other speakers in tongues appear possessed entirely and speak in a voice quite unlike their own normal range. This sort is more likely to be highly emotional in delivery and somewhat of a strain on the individual. The messages come from spiritual adepts in the astral world, although some messages allegedly come from living swamis, gurus, and mahatmas in Tibet.

Some speakers in tongues have allegedly given messages in lost languages or languages alleged to be used on other planets. Still other messages in tongues are curious mixtures of various languages, some highly formalized and grammatical in construction, other portions whimsical, to say the least.

Ministers, mediums, and occult adepts have had experiences with speaking in tongues and, like direct or automatic writing, both of which see, the messages may come at any time.

The fact that the messages are in a foreign language is offered as proof of their authenticity on the grounds that the speaker, in many instances, is barely articulate in his native language much less versed in foreign tongues.

GNOMES—Guardians of mines and quarries, these little beings were from the race of dwarfs and lived in subterranean caves and tunnels, where they dressed exclusively in grey. Light was fatal to them, turning them to stone on contact. They worked with wood and metals, having great talent in both media.

GNOSTICS—A group of religious sects who possessed transcendental knowledge which they received through written or direct revelations. Believed to exist in ancient Egypt, Gnosticism took on a new significance in the Roman Empire at the advent of Christ. The sects often employed mixtures of the Kabbalah, astrology, Christianity, and the Babylonian, Egyptian, and Indian faiths.

They relied heavily on charms, amulets, and talismans.

Several groups containing the roots of Gnosticism in their beliefs are in currency today, many allied with Theosophy, q.v.

GOBLIN—An English household spirit, generally kind and helpful, who protected his household from encroachment by strange, mysterious spirits.

GOLEM—A Hebrew legend involving the creation of a huge monster from clay and inscribing upon it the secret name of God, *Shemhamforash*, giving life to the being. As it grew before the rabbi's eyes, he became terrified at the thought of the monster's destructive potentialities and tore the life-giving name from its forehead, causing it to crumble to dust.

GOOD WOMEN–GOOD WIVES—Supernatural beings who accompany goddesses on their rounds of granting favors. Known in some quarters as intermediaries, they are said to intercede on the behalf of worthy mortals.

GOYA, FRANCISCO—Spanish artist sometimes called "The Witch's Portrait Painter," because of his magnificent work in *The Caprichos*, a series of 80 etchings. No one has represented witches more terrifyingly than he in his "Hunting for Teeth," "Sucking Children," "A Coven," "Four Witches Flying through the Air," and "A Witch Eating with Her Family."

GRAIL, THE HOLY—A large cup or platter used by Christ at the Last Supper and, later, by Joseph of Arimathea to collect the blood of Christ at the Crucifixion; it later dematerialized because of the moral impurities of its keepers. It was long the quest of knights and religious adherents. Supposedly, it would bring salvation and purity to the finder. The subject of several poems, books, and works of music of which Tennyson's "Idylls of the King," Sir Thomas Mallory's *Morte d'Arthur*, and Richard Wagner's opera *Parsifal* are prime examples.

GRAND TRINE, THE—In astrology, when two planets are four signs or 120 degrees apart and both are trined to another planet.

GREEN—The color of hope. Appears in the aura, q.v., and as an amulet, a stone with a predominantly green color will make its wearer adept in the magical arts.

GREMLINS—In American folklore, Gremlins appeared in World War II to plague airmen by impishly causing minor difficulties with aircraft. Although not malevolent, gremlins were rather amoral and did not take sides in the war, giving their victims the temporary comfort that the gremlins would be as mischievous with one side as another. Their female counterpart is a fifinella.

GRIMOIRE—A basic text in the field of black magic which begins with the advice that the user give his soul to Satan, then continues to list spells and incantations.

A general term for a book filled with information on black magic, parodies on Christianity, and invective and spells against the Kabbalah.

GRIS-GRIS—African protective amulets, which are passive and will not counter attack, as opposed to talismans which are active.

GYPSY—The name is a contraction for Egyptian and intended to include a tribe of nomads who were versed in the occult, particularly in spells, curses, and transmutations. The term is not meant to apply to actual Egyptians, rather an indeterminate country known as "Little Egypt," and variously believed to be "Transylvania" or Palestine.

GYROMANCY—Divination in which the person spins in circles, then falls to the ground. He will have an oracular vision provided he chants the proper incantations while spinning.

A variation is the drawing of an elaborate circle, divided into as many as 24 different segments, some of which are marked with Hebrew letters and corresponding to portions of the Kabbalah, others are marked according to astrological signs. Depending on which segment the spinner falls, inferences and interpretations may be made.

H

HAG—A virulent, evil-looking woman and a sometime synonym for WITCH, q.v.

HAEMATITE—A bloodstone, worn as an amulet to stop bleeding or ground into a powder and applied to the wound to staunch the flow. It was also considered valuable for rheumy, bloodshot eyes and as a cure for snake bite.

HALLUCINATION—A false sensory impression which has no basis in reality or in the spiritual world. There are hallucinations for each of the senses: smell, taste, touch, sight, and hearing. They are neither caused by supernatural nor natural agencies.

HALLUCINOGENIC—Any agent ingested into the body which may cause distortions of external reality and cause any of the senses or all of them to receive adequate stimulation to produce an hallucination. See LSD, PSYCHEDELICS.

HAND—Symbolic of strength and power; among some people, it represents God, as in medieval pictures in which Jehovah is portrayed as a hand projected from the clouds. Raised human hands may comprise invocations to God. Figures of the hand in various positions may be used for amulets, signifying strength, wisdom, godly knowledge, etc. The position of the fingers is significant:

the first and second fingers outstretched signifies a blessing; first and fourth fingers outstretched a curse. The right hand is regarded as pure and the left hand as either unclean or representing evil. See also MUDRA, PALM READING.

HANDS, LAYING ON OF—Faith healing or healing by the use of divine power and no other agency. Generally represented by the practitioner placing his or her hand on the ill or afflicted, uttering an incantation or prayer and calling for the patient to cast off illness and affliction. The practitioner allegedly has psychic or divine powers, granted through apprenticeship to another practitioner or magician, from piety or directly from a divine source. See also EMBRACE, FAITH HEALING.

HANDS, LAYING ON OF BY ENGLISH KINGS—A practice which began with Edward the Confessor and which more or less ended with Queen Anne, the power was part of the divine power invested in the royalty. Carried on by many monarchs more as a tradition, the laying on of hands genuinely interested Edward and other more religious monarchs. James I continued the practice, although embarrassed by the thought of using his hands to cure his subjects, but the majority of his subjects seemed to believe in him and the practice and so, for more political than occult reasons, James continued to offer this form of healing. William III was openly skeptical and involved himself more to continue the tradition than for any other reason. When a subject came to him for a laying on of hands to cure some ailment, William uttered a curt: "May God give you better health and more sense."

HAUNTED HOUSES—The spirits of the dead often frequent places important to the person when he was alive. If a person had been wronged in life, he was quite likely to return for belated justice. Some houses are haunted by malevolent spirits which make them unfit for habitation without prior exorcism, q.v. See also POLTERGEISTS. Other houses are haunted by friendly ghosts who become a part of the family who lives there.

HAZEL WAND—Believed to be the tree of the god Thor; in some areas of Europe this tree is still believed to have powerful occult properties, particularly of divination. The hazel rod is extremely popular for use as a divining rod by dowsers, q.v., and is considered the badge of authority of the fairies.

HECATE—The goddess ruler of the underworld, queen of all witches and patroness of the crossroads, where she frequently appeared accompanied by a pack of howling dogs and spirits. She lived in tombs. There have been many secret cults devoted to her worship; many of these exist today.

HE-GOAT—One of the forms the Devil takes, especially when visiting a coven or having intercourse with a witch. See BACHELOR.

HER—Ancient sky god represented by twin eyes which were painted on coffins and funerary equipment in ancient Egypt as a protection for the dead and a reminder of eternal life for the spirit of the departed.

HERMES TRISMEGISTUS—A name meaning "The Thrice Greatest Hermes," it was the name given by the Greeks to the Egyptian god Thoth, q.v., who was the god of occult wisdom, learning, and literature. To him is attributed the authorship of books and scrolls of divine revelation taken in dictation and interview with the gods and thus called Hermetic Scriptures. Because of the extremely sacred nature of his writings, occultists gravitated to him and he found himself the head of an intensive cycle of mystics, all of whom were quite prolific in pre-Christian times. His most famous works available are "The Perfect Sermon," and philosophical scrolls.

HEXAGRAM—The six-sided shield of Solomon, a protection against fire. Within the hexagram are written Hebrew letters of the agla, q.v. Alongside the two triangles are the letters YH and YHWN, this in Kabbalistic hexagrams, the letters being magical abbreviations of the name of God and having further power based on numerology, q.v. An extremely powerful sign either in white or black magic.

HOBGOBLIN—See GOBLIN, BROWNIES. A famous hobgoblin or benevolent spirit was Robin Goodfellow, who wandered through the forests for the purpose of helping stranded mortals.

HOCUS POCUS—Words of magical import, particularly when used as a part of an incantation. Believed to be a corruption of the Latin *hoc est corpus*, "this is the body," a phrase used by Catholic priests in the act of transubstantiation.

HOLY-MOUTH MEN—In the hierarchy of magical practitioners of the Nacirema, a North American tribe with an almost pathological horror of and fascination with the mouth. They believe the condition of the mouth has a supernatural influence on *all* relationships; if not for their mouth rituals, the teeth would fall out, the gums bleed, the jaws shrink; their friends would desert them and their lovers spurn them. A major relationship between oral and moral functions also exists.

Holy-mouth men officiate at all ritual functions of the mouth, including the daily ritual of a mouth rite in which a bundle of hog hairs are inserted into the mouth along with magical powers and moved about in a series of prescribed gestures.

The mouth is the means through which a devil or evil spirit may enter the body, causing the host irreparable damage, hence the need for constant care.

HOME, DANIELD DUNGLAS—(1833–1866) An Englishman and one of the most famous of all spiritualistic mediums; he toured the United States and widely in Europe. His greatest triumphs were in England, where he produced nearly every form of materialization, ranging from table rappings and levitation to ectoplasm and actual spirits. Although widely attended and frequently attacked, Home was never caught in fraud, a remarkable situation considering the interest in him of some of the most noted scientists and psychic researchers of the day. He was involved in an important series of seances and experiments with Sir William Crookes, q.v.

HOMEOPATHIC MAGIC—Often used synonymously with imitative magic; an extrapolation of the like produces like theory in which an attempt is made to destroy or injure an enemy by destroying or injuring an image of him. This may or may not be used in connection with contagious magic, q.v.

HOROSCOPE—A map of the heavens, charting the exact location of the sun and planets in the heavens at the precise moment of an individual's birth. It is from this map that an astrologer begins to draw inferences and divinations through reference to the influences and counter influences of the planets. See ASTROLOGY and ZODIAC, HOUSES OF.

HOUSE—In astrology, a division representing one-twelfth of the heavens. The region of a specific influence; an area in which one or more planets may be located at a given time. See ZODIAC, HOUSES OF.

HUBBARD, L. RON—American author, philosopher. A former writer of science-fiction and adventure stories, Hubbard, through an intense interest in psychology, modern science, and philosophy devised a method of treatment which would enable persons to break free of emotional restraints and develop greater abilities, powers of concentration, and willingness to cope with personal problems. This was called Dianetics, a movement with Hubbard as its leader. The movement later developed into scientology, q.v.

HUACAS—Supernatural places or objects venerated by the Incas. Not clear if the spirits actually reside in the objects, visit them occasionally, or merely endow them with certain magical powers.

HUMAN WOLVES AMONG THE NAVAHO—A belief quite similar to lycanthropy, q.v., in which an individual is invaded by the spirit of a wolf, to the exclusion of his own personality. He is driven with the same motivations and hungers of a wolf and will often exhibit characteristic psychosis and hysteria found in the tribe.

HUNS—Believed by the Germans to be the result of intercourse between women and evil spirits, and to have many witches among their number.

HUNA—A magical religion, found throughout the Pacific and scattered through South America, in which an individual may have dreams after proper ritual preparation. These dreams will come true.

HYDROMANCY—Methods of divination from water. The water may be in a dish, pond, or still body of water, although some attempts to divine from ocean tides have been noted.

HYPNOTISM—A method of inducing unconscious concentration in an individual and generally thought to play an integral part in many ritual and ceremonial beliefs. Particularly in such rites where pain is a potential—fire handling, fire walking, jabbing with needles, etc.—the individual is thought to have been either self-hypnotised or brought into the state through the help of a medicine man, priest, or drugged potion.

I

I CHING—A complex method of fortune telling and divination originated by the ancient Chinese and depending upon the interpretation of marked sticks which are cast by the person wishing information. Entire books have been written on the possible interpretations of the patterns of sticks after they are cast. Since the individual tossing the sticks has great personal control over the amount of force with which they are thrown, this method of telling fortune is regarded as quite an accurate personal reflection. Still quite popular among Orientals and Occidentals today.

ICTHYOMANCY—Divination by means of the entrails of a fish.

ILLUMINATI—Those occult persons who are able to manifest enough power to cause luminescent glowings in their auras.

IMHOTEP—An Egyptian god who was frequently called upon to offer assistance in cases of exorcism.

IMMORTALITY—The state of deathlessness; the great quest of mankind. The Fountain of Youth, the Fountain of Life, various elixirs, balms, and incantations are said to grant this gift to mortals. It is also granted to some mortals by gods, elevating the status considerably. It is important to note that all super-beings are not necessarily immortal.

INCUBUS—A spirit which assumes the likeness of men in order to have sexual intercourse with human females, a function often performed as the woman sleeps and the reality of which is covered by the belief that the woman

77

was having an erotic dream. If she is impregnated by this union, she will give birth to a child who is the property of the forces of darkness. Accounts of a strong belief in this phenomenon, and belief in its actuality, are on record throughout Europe and Asia.

INEFFABLE—That which is too awful (literally) to be spoken aloud. Thus such abbreviations as YH and YVH for the Hebrew god, similar powers for corresponding gods, and charms in other religions. One consequence for uttering such a word might be found in the Golem, q.v.

INK—A red or black ink over which certain incantations were chanted was the usual choice for writing magical formulas, especially by sorcerers, but in a few cases where the formula was felt to have an especial power, green ink was used. In some mystic rites involving the pledge of the soul, human blood was used as an ink, particularly for signatures.

INNER MAN—Also called spiritual body and corpus glorification; terms for the Godhead which dwells in each man. The mystics of all major religions have reported experiences of seeing the God within. They also concur in the belief that the inner man radiates a light which may be discernible. The ancient Egyptians called this ba, or the soul of man. They likened it to a star and represented it in hieroglyphics as such.

INSUFFLATION—Healing by means of breath. An adept or a medicine man breathes hot or cold air on the patient, according to the type of cure necessary. Warm insufflation should be applied first to the feet of the patient, then moved upwards toward the source of trouble. It is used to restore good circulation and dispel depressions. Cold insufflation should be initiated at the top of the head, then brought downward; it heals congestions and soothes pain.

INTUITION—In occult terms, a message from an extra-sensory source.

INVOCATIONS—An incantation for the specific purpose of summoning a supernatural being or agency; an occult prayer to add strength to a spell.

IRON—A strong defense against fairies. In some areas, bags filled with iron ore and worn as an amulet were considered powerful against the evil eye.

ISIS—The greatest and most powerful of Egyptian goddesses; her worship spread to other countries via mystical cults and persists to this day. Some of her ancient titles suggest her many attributes: She of the many names, She who is from the beginning, She who is without end, the only true bestower of life.

IX—One of four Mayan gods which held up the earth. See BACABS.

J

JACINTH—A stone worn as an amulet against lightning and disorders of the heart; it attracts honor, wisdom, and prudence, and is often used in ground form as a medicine for an internal disorder connected with bleeding.

JACOB'S LADDER—A Kabbalistic view of a rainbow presented to Jacob in a divine dream and bringing with it the portents of alchemy and the potential powers alchemists could unleash.

JADE—Used as an amulet to assist women in childbirth and to help men become victorious in battle. It also protected the wearer from lightning. In China, used by businessmen as a divination medium, particularly in business matters. In Mexico, sometimes used as a knife blade for human sacrifices made by the Mayans.

JASPER—A semi-precious stone to be used as an amulet, either in polished form or with scratched inscriptions of charms. Allegedly strengthens the intellect and prevents fevers, nightmares, and epilepsy seizures.

JAWBONE—In ancient Egypt and modern Africa there are widespread beliefs that the ghost of a recently departed person will attach itself to the jawbone after death. Thus, a jawbone becomes a spiritual wand, a weapon with supposed invincibility and a shrine.

JEALOUSY—One of the most common motives for the practice of black magic, especially the evil eye.

JET—This stone, when ground into a powder and tossed into a fire drives away poisonous snakes and lizards. Italian women wear beatles carved from jet as a protection from the evil eye.

JETTATURA—The power of the evil eye, according to Southern Italians and Sicilians.

JINN—Arabian spirits who sprang from fire and ruled the earth for thousands of years before the advent of Adam. They have the power to make themselves visible or invisible at will, or to assume the form of animals. They have some ability at divination, but they are also subject to the powers of incantations and rituals.

JOURNEY OF THE SOUL—Akin to clairvoyance and astral flight except that the sensitive travels in his spirit body and observes at the scene of the action, then returns back to the physical body rather than remaining in the physical body and "seeing" what is beyond the reach of his physical eyes.

JUJU MAN—African priest of black magic; they practice cannibalism, are initiated with a drink of blood and excreta, have the power to change a man's face so radically that his own mother would not recognize him.

They also have the ability to change into birds and fly away from danger.

JUNG, CARL GUSTAV—(1875–1964) A Swiss psychologist and disciple of Freud; one of the first modern men of science to give healthy speculation to occultism and spirituality. He believed in the presence of a collective unconsciousness, which seemed to suggest, at the very least, the passing of racial traits, myths, and memories by instinct.

JUNIPER—A small evergreen tree used in a manner similar to that of water witching or dowsing, for the location of lost objects. Supposedly powerful in recalling lost sheep.

JUPITER—A Roman god ruling over all others. In astrology, a planet and house. See ZODIAC, HOUSES OF.

K

KA—A spiritual or astral double provided for every mortal at birth and also found in animals and inanimate objects. It is a spiritual essence which might also be linked to the genetic terms of genes and chromosomes, thanks to the individualistic quality it imparts to its host.

KABBALAH—A Hebrew system of theosophy; doctrines of mystical religion with strong traditional foundations. It is a mainstem of Hebrew occult beliefs. Because of its suppression by Jewish orthodoxy, it is impossible to estimate how widely it is practiced, but during the Middle Ages, many of the greatest sorcerers followed this book of mystical rituals, incantations and spells that allegedly had effect over all forms of matter. See THEOSOPHY.

KACHINAS—In American Indian religions, particularly among Hopi, Navaho, and Zuni, they were spirits of the dead or representatives of gods who appear from the underworld and join in at ceremonial dances and rituals. Essentially benevolent spirits, governing all important aspects of rain, wind, sun, fertility, animals, crops, etc., they may have vindictive missions if they have not been properly honored.

Also invisible spirits which may enter the bodies of properly dressed and ritually cleansed mortals at ceremonials and dances.

Dolls carved from cottonwood roots in the images of the various kachinas are given to the young to use as toys and as the first step in teaching them the function and importance of these powerful religious figures.

KALI—The Hindu goddess of life and death. Kali dances creation into being, but when she accidentally touches Siva, the supreme Godhead, all creation stops. Then, only God exists until Kali stirs and begins dancing again. This concept, older than Christianity or Judaism, is strangely akin to the modern astronomer's theory of pulsing expansion and collapse of the universe. Kali is also responsible for individual life and death. For this reason, there have been many erotic and homicidal cults dedicated to her. The infamous Thugee sect believed Kali must be fed with human lives.

KAN—One of four important Mayan gods. See BACABS.

KANEA—Magic squares used by Kabbalists as amulets. Each Kanea is associated with an astrological planet and a demon. In letters of numerical significance, they contain the essence of God.

KARMA—In Brahmanism, Buddhism, Theosophy, and various occult beliefs, a word meaning action and referring to the spiritual life being lived by the individual or the spiritual lives already lived by the individual. A result of both good and evil actions and the inevitable consequences in this life or the next until the individual progresses beyond good and evil and into God, where he then escapes the "wheel" of karma.

KAVA—A narcotic beverage of the South Pacific Islands. It is believed to have been originated by a powerful deity and is prepared by young men and women who chew the roots and stem of the plant, then spit the juice into a large bowl of highly polished wood which is never washed.

KETEB—The noonday devil, greatly feared by followers of the Kabbalah as a great source of evil and danger.

KHAIB—The Egyptian name for the shadow which sometimes left the body to lead a life of its own.

KING'S EVIL—A disease known as scrofula, which was supposed to be cured with the most ease by laying on of hands by a king. See HANDS, LAYING ON OF BY ENGLISH KINGS.

KINGS—Often chief priest-sorcerer and, hence, powerfully sacred. Some kings were said to be so filled with mystical power that only a selected few people could touch them without ill effects, a possible explanation for brother-sister marriages of Egypt and Hawaii.

KISCHUPH—The part of the Kabbalah which deals with magic and sorcery. It contains the knowledge for causing illness and death by magic, and for disguising one's self in the shape of an animal or for embarking on spiritual travel.

KISS—Used by some witches and sorcerers to gain power over a victim; supposedly effective because a portion of a person's soul or spirit mingles with the one who is kissing him. See also EMBRACE.

KNOTS—Muslim - magicians tie knots as they say their incantations, hence the designation, Blowers on Knots. The breath of the magician is imbued with magical powers, giving the rope of cord additional power. It is said that on one occasion a sorcerer and his two witch daughters cast a spell on Mohammed by tying eleven knots in a cord. The prophet would have died if God had not intervened on his behalf.

KOLA—A stimulant. Both physical strength and mental alertness are improved by chewing. In Africa, natives claim it also stimulates sexual excitement and increases capacities. Kola nuts must be included in every dowry and they are burned with each corpse.

KOONS SPIRIT ROOM—A room with 16 and 12 foot dimensions, built by Jonathan Koons and used only for seances. In the middle of the nineteenth century, Koons, a spiritualist, and his son were able to make some startling contacts with the spirit world in this construction. The explanation offered for the effectiveness was the proportions of the room and its compatability for vibrations.

KUNDJE—A benevolent form of magic as expressed in the New Guinea Highlands. A characteristic is the powerful effect in bringing good results to the user and danger to those it is used against.

KUTHUN—A scapular, amulet, pincushion, letter, book, or any paper with written incantations given by a witch at the time of her death to another witch; an inheritance given by a dying witch to another witch or her apprentice. A legacy making a neophyte witch fulfilled in her powers.

L

LACERATIONS—Self-inflicted cuts or wounds are frequently used in the trance state of the witch doctor and priest. They are often an integral part of mystical worship. Many Catholic saints lacerated their bodies. In Mexico today, there are cults whose followers lacerate their bodies with cactus whips. In general, the laceration is to show subjugation, or the ability to ignore pain. See also PAIN.

LAMASHTU—An especially powerful and evil female demon. She is often pictured holding a snake in each hand while she suckles a jackal. Her face strikes horror in all who glimpse it, but she especially hates and attacks young children and pregnant women.

LAND OF THE DEAD, THE—Among peoples of the spirit world, it is regarded as a world different from the world of the living, but it is not like the concepts of heaven or hell.

LAPIS LAZULI—A semi-precious stone used for carving scarabs and images of God. Because of its apparent beauty, it is believed that the gods enjoy inhabiting the stone and investing it with magical powers.

LATIPSO—A medicine temple employed by shamans of the Nacerima, a North American group of Indians covering a wide area. Used in a portion of the holy-mouth rites, q.v.

LAUREL—A tree whose leaves give men protection against evil spirits. Also used to crown Greek and Roman royalty, particularly those who were elevated to a divine status. A symbol of victory, power, divinity and especial favor from the gods. The laurel leaf, when soaked in water, presented an allegedly powerful protective elixir.

LEGION—The world of spirits located between earth and heaven. Not to be confused with Hell.

LEFT SIDE—Universally considered impure and unlucky. Priests and worshippers traditionally make their offerings with the right hand while witches and sorcerers make offers to the devil with the left hand.

LEMURIA—A lost continent. See MU.

LENT—In Catholic Europe, a dangerous birthtime. A person born during Lent has the ability to see ghosts and could be frightened to death.

LEO—In astrology, the sign represented by the Lion. See ZODIAC, HOUSES OF.

LEONARD, GLADYS OSBORNE—(1882–1964) An English medium who became one of the best documented of all time. She held sittings for over fifty years, often with prominent psychical researchers, some of whom sat with her regularly, over periods of ten or twenty years. Never was there any question of fraud or insincerity in connection with her spiritual work.

LEPRECHAUNS—A tribe of Irish fairies appearing as a little man of approximately two feet in height, generally dressed in a cocked hat, laced coat, knickers, and shoes with silver buckles. A shoemaker by trade, he was known to haunt wine cellars. If he found good drinking, he was likely to show the house where he stayed amazing services and aids, much on the order of the brownies, q.v.

LETTERS—Each letter of the alphabet has its own mystical power thus amulets may have additional power because of the letters inscribed on them for yet other purposes.

LE VESQUE, G. VICTOR—Eighteenth century Canadian spiritualist and leader of a faith healing cult involving aspects of the Kabbalah, Theosophy, and mysticism. The favored amulet was that of a black cat and Le Vesque was famous for a home-brew type potion of considerable alcoholic content.

LEVITATION—The act of rising from the ground and floating through the air without mechanical aids. May apply to humans, animals, and inanimate objects, the latter of which are caused to levitate by a force known as psychokinesis, q.v.

Accounts of levitation are world wide and come from

many different religions and magical systems. The Hindus claim levitation may be learned by the faithful through the performance of proper yoga exercises. The Roman Catholic church has documented some of their mystically oriented saints levitating while experiencing divine ecstasy. Similarly, Tibetan Buddhism is filled with accounts of their holy llamas levitating.

In seances, a frequent feat of a physical medium, who may levitate or cause objects to levitate. See APPORTS.

The noted anthropologist Malinowski records accounts of levitating witches in the Trobriand Islands of the South Pacific.

LIBATION SLAB—An altar or table on which offerings are placed or poured.

LIBRA—In astrology, a sign represented by scales or a balance. See ZODIAC, HOUSES OF.

LIFE—As awareness of self, a foundation of occult and religious practices whose ultimate purpose is extending and preserving individual consciousness and insuring the existence of the soul in the next world.

LIGHTNING, FORKED—An ancient symbol of power, related to the cross and swastika, both of which see.

LILITH—The demon wife Adam enjoyed before God created Eve.

LINES—In palmistry, divisions of the hand denoting characteristics and attributes. Thus, the line of life, a line flanking the thumb. The line of the heel joins life line directly with first finger. The line of fate transverses the center of the hand. The line of fortune is parallel to and below the line of fate. The line of heart is parallel to the line of the heel.

LION, HEAD OF—A symbol of strength, particularly as an amulet.

LITANY—A song or chant of worship; distinct from an

invocation in that it does not beckon God to the worshiper but sends the worshipper to Him.

LIVER, DIVINATION BY—The ancient Hebrews and Babylonians claimed the use of divination by means of the liver of a cow or goat had been invented by the gods.

LOKI—An evil force, the son of a being whose job it was to ferry dead souls over the waters of the underworld. A being of viciousness and cunning, he is considered a personification of the destructive elements of fire.

LOTUS—An Asian water plant whose flower is known for its beauty. Hence the word has come to be synonymous with beauty. A favorite pedestal or throne for the Indian deities. The various emotional, intellectual, and spiritual centers in the human body are symbolized by the lotus. In yoga, the lotus position is a cross-legged posture in which the instep of both feet rests on the opposite thigh and the hands are cupped in the lap as a strong aid to meditation.

LOTS, DRAWING OF—One of the oldest forms of divination, which still survives in every schoolyard in the Western world. In ancient Rome and Gaul the lots were made of wood, bone, and ivory.

LOVE AMULET—Special words written on copper with ink made from crushed lotus blossoms.

LOVE APPLES—Mandrake roots used by ancient and modern magicians in making love philtres.

LOVE POTIONS, PHILTRES—Belief in these has been widespread and strong. The formulas differ, but one ingredient which is common to them all is a bit of hair or clothing from the person to be bewitched. See CONTAGIOUS MAGIC, FETISHES.

LSD-25, LYSERGIC ACID DIETHYLAMIDE—The most famous of all psychedelic or consciousness expanding drugs. One of the earliest known LSD experiences came in 1943, when a Swiss pharmacist was conducting experiments with ergot, a spur-shaped fungus which grows on rye, oats, and other grains. Hoffman experienced hallucinations which he finally ascribed to the drug. Later experimentation resulted in larger doses which produced massive hallucinations in Hoffman and reactions in others which ranged from mystical-religious to pseudopsychotic. Many occult persons have claimed to have had occult encounters, visions, and long astral flights under its influence. Although physiologic addiction to the compound is unlikely, the reactions to it cannot be controlled to a great extent. Some occultists have found particularly meaningful mystical and occult experiences by a prior preparation with the Tibetian *Book of the Dead*. Because of the highly unpredictable nature of the drug, some states are passing laws making its possession a felony, and further investigation reveals the simplicity with which anyone familiar with chemistry may synthesize it.

LUCIFER—The bearer of light, an angel whose pride caused him to revolt against God. For the gift of a mouse, he would appear to magicians and do their bidding. His name is the first to be invoked in the witches' sabbath.

LUCK—A quality of fortuitous circumstance which many believe to be controlled by magic. See FORTUNE.

LYCANTHROPY—The transformation of a human being into a wolf, or werewolf, for evil purposes. The transformation is usually physical, in which case the being may return to his human physical form on most occasions, generally being called into his lupine shape at the sight of the full moon, or at the behest of a witch. In some cases, the spirit double is also changed, making it problematical whether or not the werewolf may return to his physical body as a human.

Lycanthropy goes hand-in-hand with homicide and cannibalism, the afflicted person either tearing out the throats of his victims and occasionally feasting on their blood or, in the manner of a vampire, biting them in such a way as to change them into a werewolf.

See also, HUMAN WOLVES AMONG THE NAVAHO.

M

MACUMBA—Brazilian native witchcraft; a form of voodoo, q.v.

MACROCOSM—A six-pointed star which is formed with two triangles; the sacred seal of Solomon representing the infinite and the absolute. One of the two major Kabbalistic symbols into which all other magical signs may be reduced, the basis on which spiritual entities may be called into service by means of incantations over signs.

MACROPROSOPUS—One of the four Kabbalistic signs for the basic elements, this represents the magic of earth.

MADABI—To transmute pieces of matter. A belief among the Lobedu of Transvaal, it is a form of sympathetic magic in which the skin of an animal, for instance, may be turned into the entire animal.

MAGI—Ancient priests in Persia and followers of the religion of Zoroaster. Renowned for their wisdom, humanity, and abilities in the occult.

MAGIC—The science of the supernatural; also referred to as the art of the supernatural. There is evidence to suggest that magic predates religion in terms of man's participation. Some aspects of magic and religion are indistinguishable, but the essential difference is that magic forces or manipulates the supernatural to do man's bidding. The witch doctor, magician, and sorcerer use ritual and incantations which effect the supernatural as automatic and unfailing agencies over the entire person. In addition to the different areas of magic, there is the magic of the individual. Some people have greater capacity to work magic than others.

White magic is used to benefit others; black magic is used to do harm. These terms are not as objective as they might appear, depending on the interpretation of what is beneficial.

MAGICAL DIAGRAMS—Geometric designs which symbolize the mysteries of creation or represent a deity. They are used to conjure and enjoin and evoke. The most powerful diagrams are the triangle, the symbol of truth; the shield of Solomon, symbol of the macrocosm; the Tehayra, symbol of the four elements; and the pentegram, which is symbolic of the microcosm. With one point in the ascendant, it is the sign of Christ, but with two points ascending, it is the sign of Satan. The pentegram is said to be the most powerful diagram for conjuring demons and spirits.

MAGICAL FRIGHT—A belief in the effects of certain magical spells. See SUSTO, ESPANTO.

MAGICAL INSTRUMENTS—Equipment used in the performing of magical rituals. Among them are the altar, the chalice, the censer, lamp, sword or rod, the trident, fire, consecrated oil, water, incense, candles, and offerings.

MAGICAL MIRRORS—There are three kinds; the mirror of the future, which is made from well water or river water and placed in an especially constructed vessel; the mirror of the present, made from a magic ink which is held in the sorcerer's hand; and the mirror of character, which is made from a polished stone and reflects the condition of the soul.

MAGICAL NUMBERS—Certain numbers and combinations have power because they represent supernatural mysteries. See NUMEROLOGY.

MAGICAL VESTMENTS—Special clothing which imparts power to magical ritual. In Africa, most witch doctors perform their magic while naked, except for an especially made loin cloth. Western magicians generally wear elaborate robes of special material and symbolic colors.

MANA—A supernatural power which possesses things and people to varying degrees. See TABOO. Like electricity, mana is neither good nor evil in itself, but may be used for either purpose. Like electricity, it is sometimes difficult to harness, but worth the effort.

MANDRAKE—One of the most mysterious and romanticized of all plants, a humanoid cry is said to be heard when this valuable addition to the occult pharmacology is pulled from the ground, the shriek supposedly the cry of jealous spirits who dwell within. The mandrake has a long history of use as an aphrodisiac in ancient Egypt, through Hippocrates and into the present day in Iran and Iraq. Also used an an anesthetic by the Romans, an aid to conception by the Germans. Known in some areas as Devil's Apples.

MALEFICUM—Injury to person, life or property through supernatural means.

MALPHAS—A demon whose natural shape is that of a large raven. When he takes a human form, he has a very hoarse voice. It is difficult to deal with the malphas because he enjoys deception, which he extends even to his worshippers.

MARS, INFLUENCE OF—Creates aggressive personalities, reckless and violent natures, iron wills, and great ambitions. See ASTROLOGY, and ZODIAC, HOUSES OF.

MATERIALISM—Making a visible and palpable body or part by a spirit through the agency of a medium at a seance.

MEDICINE—Especially among American Indians and African tribes, medicine is used synonymously with magic, but this gives it an even more religious significance. In another sense, medicine may be considered a series of elements, charms, and amulets which work well for an individual or clan. Hence, bad medicine is anything working against the individual or clan, or against good medicine which they possess.

MEDICINE DREAM—Among American Indians, particularly plains Indians, a period of ritual initiation into the adult mysteries and status of the tribe and the religion. Generally, the participant must cleanse and purify himself with sweat baths, abstention from sexual relations, and a period of fasting. He must set out from the tribe, wandering until he reaches a state of near delirium, at which time it is believed he will have dreams and experiences which will shape his future. These dreams and experiences—usually with animals or birds who seem to talk to the individual—are reported to the tribal medicine man, who interprets them, assigns a medicine name to the individual, and suggests various items which should properly be carried in the individual's medicine bundle or worn as an amulet.

MEDICINE MAN—A witch doctor, shaman, magician, etc. Usually a person who has innate powers which he has increased by studying magical ritual and incantation. A person who applies knowledge of the supernatural for a result obtained through black or white magic.

MEDIUM—Also called sensitive; a person with the capacity to communicate with the dead and with the spirit world to an unusual degree. Communication is generally achieved by the medium allowing the spirits the temporary use of his body.

MEDUSA—A mortal with hair of writhing serpents and a face so horrible that the beholder was turned to stone.

MERCURY—As an influence in astrology, gives a man excellent memory, great verbal skills, artistic ability, enthusiasm, capriciousness, and short-range vision.

MERMAIDS—Mythological female beings with the lower portion of their bodies being fishlike, their upper bodies being human. Also mermen, similarly constructed. Essentially benevolent, their function was to assist mortals when at sea. Some cases show mermaids and mermen were assigned their form through an incantation and, unknown to them, the incantation also imparted the ability to lure men into loving them.

METROSCOPY—The relation of the human forehead to the planets, invented by Cardano, an Italian mathematician, who anticipated phrenology, q.v., by dividing the forehead into zones and assigning a planetary influence to each. Cardano insisted his subjects have their readings done in the morning, before breakfast, an interesting, if unintentional relationship to the present technique for taking basal metabolism.

MICROCOSM—Literally, a microscopic world or worlds; figuratively the worlds which exist within our world. Symbolized by the five pointed star. See MAGICAL DIAGRAMS.

MOLOCH—A demon who devours infants.

MONAD—In theosophy, a divine spark which fires up the mental body, astral body, and personality and is destroyed at death, only to return to the logos as a part of the process of reincarnation, to come forth again in a new life.

MOON, INFLUENCE OF—Creates happy marriages, religious sensibilities, secretive natures, and industrious work habits.

MOONSTONE—A semi-precious stone which protects the wearer against epilepsy. Also assists plant growth.

MU, LOST CONTINENT OF—A supposed continent which once existed in the Pacific Ocean and which, thousands of years ago, sank below the surface, leaving only tiny outcroppings which are supposedly now the South Pacific Islands. The alleged inhabitants of this highly advanced culture were supposedly related to the Mayans and Incas. Of this civilization, it is said that they advanced too far for mortals and thus, to silence them, their continent was deluged, forcing the survivors to scatter. Also called LEMURIA.

MUDRA—Particularly in Hindu, yoga, and mystical religions, a means of using the hands and fingers in various positions to represent prayers. Some mudras, accompanied by the proper concentration, may lead the individual into mystical experiences.

MULUC—One of four Mayan gods. See BACABS.

MUSES—The powerful god Zeus had nine daughters by Mnemosyne, all of whom became goddesses in their own right, each taking a branch of the arts or sciences on which to bestow particular blessing and patronage. Their worship originated with the Thracians, who were very much aware of the muses and who engaged in elaborate ritual to secure their blessing or assistance in their artistic and scientific endeavor. The muses were: Calliope, eloquence and epic poetry; Clio, history; Euterpe, music and lyric poetry; Melpomene, tragedy; Terpsichore, dancing; Erato, love poetry; Polyhymnia, sacred poetry; Thalia, comedy and pastoral poetry; Urania, astronomy.

MUSHROOM MADNESS—Because of the psychedelic content of many mushrooms, users often become temporarily mad or subject to delusion or hallucination. Modern psychiatrists agree that the state is a pseudo-psychosis.

MYOMANCY—Divination with rodents. Either the entrails are used or the rodent is placed in a square or circle on which significant numbers or letters are written. The numbers over which the rodent scurries influence the divination.

MYSTERIES—Originally the rites of secret cults in ancient Greece; of pre-Hellenic origin. A combination of fertility rites and black magic involving animal sacrifice and sexual orgy. Now commonly any private ritual, formula, incantation, symbolism spell, or password belonging to a group which has a restricted membership.

MYSTICISM—The practice of certain holy men of communicating the mergence with God. All religions have their mystics and, surprisingly enough, regardless of how the religions vary, the mystical experiences seem to be quite similar. Mystics generally tend to accept each other, even when they come from opposing religious sects. See *Mysticism for the Millions,* by Norman Winski.

N

NIAD—Nymphs of rivers, brooks, and springs. See also NYMPHS.

NAIL CLIPPINGS—Because of the nature of contagious magic, q.v., nail parings, bits of hair, spittle, excreta, etc. give the sorcerer power over the person they once were a part of. Nail clippings are popular since they may be collected without arousing suspicion.

NAME, POWER OF—Certain names have intrinsic magical power. See WORD, MANA.

NARCOTICS—Have been used by witch doctors to help them get through to the supernatural world. Whether narcotics actually have this power or whether they have only the power to deceive is still a matter of debate. Aldous Huxley expressed belief that they were effective tools for developing mystical powers.

NATURE SPIRIT—Includes sylphs, gnomes, undines, and salamanders; they are mischievous and unpredictable, sometimes aiding man, sometimes doing him harm. Theosophists claim they are beings whose bodies are made of astral matter.

NATURAL WORLD—The natural world is that which can be perceived and manipulated by animals and humans of little or average power. Thus, water belongs to the natural world and the elixir of life belongs to the numinous world.

NECKLACES—Originally and still used as an unusually powerful amulet. Beads of bloodstone, garnet, mother of pearl (nacre), crystal, and ivory have special powers of protection. Among the Egyptians, these semi- and precious stones were arranged so that the first letters of their names would spell out magical words, thus adding additional powers.

NECROMANCY—Divination by means of ghosts. A necromancer may summon spirits and compel them to perform services or give him information. Contrasted to a medium, who is merely possessed by spirits, who may leave his presence at any time they desire.

NEOPHYTE—A novice or apprentice magician, necromancer, or sorcerer.

NEW BIRTH—A frequent initiation ceremony. First the neophyte goes through a ritual death ceremony and then is reborn again. Frequently, his body is literally pushed through the legs of a priestess who cries as though undergoing the agonies of labor. The initiate, thus "reborn", has a new set of parents assigned to him in addition to his natural parents; these are his magical or spiritual parents, and the extent of the neophyte's powers depend on the power of his sponsoring magical parents.

NEW THOUGHT—A forerunner and anticipation of Christian Science, developed by Phineas Parkhurst Quimby, q.v., in which aspects of mesmerism (hypnotism) and faith healing were linked to a process called animal magnetism. This aspect is closely akin to sympathetic magic and alleged that illness could be drawn from an unhealthy person by a well person. A combination of hypnotism, laying on of hands and positive thinking pep talks were given the patient as a cure.

NGAMA—A medicine man and member of the Ndembo Secret Society of the Lower Congo. Called "The Knowing Ones" because of their wide range of magic ritual, healing abilities, and power over the earthly elements.

NIGHTMARE—A bad dream believed by occultists to be caused by a witch, hence a person with repeated nightmares is said to be hag-ridden. An occasional nightmare signifies the encounter of a demon or witch by the spirit of the sleeper, or the memory of an encounter while in astral flight.

NIGHTWALKER—Witches, demons, and all evil beings who deal in black magic perform better in the dark. Lightness has mana, q.v., for good but it is taboo for evil. Thus, a nightwalker is a malevolent spirit on a nefarious mission at night.

NINE—A powerful mystical number, as complete as the number three, q.v., and therefore as important. It is the double triad. There are nine muses, nine orders of angels, nine orders of devils, and nine-fold gate of hell, and the nine-day period in which Satan and his angels fell from grace in heaven.

NINTH HOUSE—In astrology, the house dealing with ideas, communication, and creativity. See ZODIAC, HOUSES OF.

NOCTURNAL RELIGIONS—A euphemism for witchcraft, employed because of the dread some people have of mentioning the word witch. Similar in concept to euphemisms for the true name of God or of powerful spirits both good and evil.

NOISE—All professions which contact the spirit world, whether they be mediums, necromancers, or priests, claim that noise frightens away the spirits. For this reason, absolute quiet is necessary as a seance is begun. And for this reason, a great deal of noise is made when attempting to dispell bewitched persons or places.

NOSTRADAMUS—(1503-1566) A French physician and mathematician who turned to astrology, then produced a tremendous bulk of prophetic material, extending from his own times well into the twenty-first century. Although his prophecies were written in a more or less allegorical verse that is criticised as being too indefinite, occultists who have kept records of his predictions say he has had an amazingly high average of successes with his predictions. His projections for the dates of World Wars I and II came within ten years of each actual event.

NUMEROLOGY—A method of divination by interpreting numbers. This may be simple or complex, based on the numerical influence of days of the week, months of the year, etc., of numbers appearing in dreams, of the number of times an incantation is recited, *ad. inf.* Many numerologists believe conscious and unconscious thoughts are governed by numbers, thus a number becomes a symbol of an occult, mystical, or current event. The total of numbers in an individual or god's name gives information on his personality, powers, and future fortunes.

Several great mystics and occultists have written works in which the significance of numbers is detailed. A method of using numerology is to ask the subject for the first three numbers which comes to his mind. Each of these numbers will have bearing on the past, present, and future and when totalled, may give the numerologist a complete personality reading.

In general, the numbers are reduced by addition to the basics of 1 to 9.

NUMINOUS—Sacred and mysterious because of the powerful relationship with the mysterious and supernatural. Magic, religion, and their practitioners are part of the numinous world as opposed to the physical world. Also used as numinous to signify unworldly, mystical, or magical.

O

OAK—Both the Druids and the Hebrews felt this tree was sacred. The Druids worshipped the spirit of the tree and performed propitiatary and magical rites under it. Many Semitic idols were carved from oak to impart greater effectiveness to them; thus some primitives where Christianity has made an appearance will deliberately make carvings of Christ or the saints from oak.

Used as a toothache cure, oak was placed into a cavity made by a nail.

OAK APPLES—A brown plum-sized pod which grows on oaks; used to test fascination of infants by witches and other spirits. An oak apple was placed in a bowl of water under the crib of the infant. If the oak apple floated, this was considered evidence of fascination or possible possession.

OATH—A ritualistic declaration of intent based on an allegiance to God or a spirit. Usually given with the clear-cut implication that the utterer of the oath will be punished if he breaks his word.

OBEAH—The witchcraft practices of the West Indies. An obeah man practices black magic, specializing in cursing witching and killing.

OBELISK—A tall, four-sided pillar bearing hieroglyphics

usually sacred in nature. A shrine of mystical or religious power.

OBJECTS OF INTRUSION—A spiritual cause of disease. According to the theory, a foreign element finds its way to the flesh of a human. This element may be activated by a spell or curse. Unless an "operation" is quickly performed, the patient rapidly grows worse and dies. However, objective observers have suspected these operations are matters of sleight of hand or trickery, and the object of the entire theory is supposedly based more on suggestion than reality.

OBLATION—An offering or sacrifice, both of which see.

OBEDIENCE—God and the Devil require absolute obedience from their followers on pain of abandonment. The spirits, however, believe only in temporal obediences. There are spells which supposedly elicit obedience to man from the spirits. These, also, are temporal.

OCHRE—A color ranging in hue from saffron yellow to red gold. Traditionally, the color of Hindu and Buddhist monks' robes. Thought to have qualities of contemplativeness, piety, and mystical powers.

OCCULT—From a Latin derivation of concealed or to cover over; the hidden, secret, esoteric, and mysterious arts which are beyond human understanding. Certain mystic arts such as divination, astrology, alchemy, magic, etc., hence forces or powers which cause the occult to take place.

ODYLLIC FORCE—Perceptible only to sensitives and occultists, odyllic force is the subtle energy which issues from every substance in the universe, and which may be harnessed for greater powers in performing the magical, mystic, or occult arts.

OFFERINGS—Gifts to the gods and spirits, usually left or given as a part of a ceremony. Generally, the various gods and spirits require gifts which are especially appropriate to them. The worshipper traditionally offers the Hindu god Shiva water and green leaves; the Aztec gods demanded offerings of human lives, etc. Many religions believe the gods take the spiritual substance of food offerings into the god-head. See PRASAD.

OGRES—Enormous beings of humanoid appearance and great ugliness, with strength proportionate to their huge size. They are not immortal and may be killed by a sufficiently powerful blow. Most ogres hate human beings and willingly become malevolent agents against them. In mythology, many mortals and folk heroes have proven their mettle by killing ogres.

OIIK—The demons of the Nanchi in the Congo. These evil spirits cause sickness, death, and earthquake.

OINTMENT—A part of the pharmacology of magic. An oil, unguent, or compound to be applied to the body or to an amulet or inanimate object to impart magical powers, curses, or cures. Some ointments may cause invisibility, visions of the past or future, superhuman strength, instant healing, etc. The ointment of the black mass is said to have as its base the fat of children or of slightly rotted corpses, hence the popularity of grave robbing and child stealing.

OLD SCRATCH—A euphemism for the Devil, possibly because of the belief that he could be summoned by scratching the appropriate design in a pentagram.

OM—The most powerful of seed words, it is used by both Hindus and Tibetan Buddhists. A potent psychic force extracted from the holy scriptures.

OMEN—A sign which has predictive value. Many priests have lexicons or lists of private omens and use them in the service of the community. Often, a priest or medicine man was judged by the number of omens at his disposal, and not infrequently, he was judged by the effectiveness with which he read them.

ONE—A sacred and powerful number because of its relation to the concepts of power, individuality, incorruptibility, and to God.

ONEIROMANCY—An interpretation of dreams which specifically excludes the use of numbers.

ONIMANCY—Divination by aid of the fingernails. The diviner reads the amount of moon showing and any spots which may appear.

ONION—The ancient Egyptians regarded the onion as a symbol of the universe. Their physicians claimed for it miraculous abilities to absorb poison. A poultice of peeled onion slices applied to the victim's stomach would quickly invalidate the effect of most poisons, potions, and philtres.

ONOMANCY—Divination with the aid of the name of the individual. See also WORDS.

ONYX—An unlucky stone, to be avoided or given to enemies. It causes warfare, hatred between friends, and nightmares.

OOSCOPY—Divination with the aid of eggs. Pregnant women could determine the sex of their child by keeping a fertilized egg between their breasts until it hatched. The sex of the chick would determine the sex of the child when born.

OPAL—A semi-precious stone; although it cures and prevents diseases of the eye, in evil hands it can cause the curse of the evil eye to become strengthened.

ORACLES—The shrine where one of the gods possesses the presiding priest or priestess and speaks through them to humans, often giving valuable information for the future. As an inanimate object, something which has been affected by a god for the purpose of presenting an omen to a diviner.

ORDEAL, TRIAL BY—Divination of guilt or innocence by

means or torture, danger or physical reaction. Variations of this practice have been used in nearly every country. The Chinese required a suspect to spit a mouthful of rice. The patterns of the rice would provide information of guilt or innocence. The virginity of the Vestal Virgins was tested with a requirement to carry water in a sieve. If the sieve leaked, the woman was judged to have lost her innocence and was, accordingly, killed. The Germanic tribes, including the Angles and Saxons, had a suspect pull a red-hot poker from a fire. If the suspect's hand was burned, he was judged guilty. The theory behind this practice was that the trial would inflict pain on the normal person and thus, if a suspect were innocent, the intervention of the gods on his behalf would be a clear indication of his status. During the Inquisition, this practice was carried to extreme, sadistic ends and it is from trial by ordeal that the modern legal concept comes of innocence until guilt is proven.

ORBS—In astrology, the space found between planets which aspect one another.

ORKOIYOT—Modern African witch doctors whose mana are so powerful that they may not be touched by other humans without consequence. They divine by casting lots, by reading the entrails of a goat, by drunken visions, and by dreams. Their service may be bought in a manner similar to paying for the services of a physician. They cure spells and sicknesses.

OSIRIS—The god incarnate of the Egyptians. Like Christ, he was born of a woman, died, and was resurrected. He had extensive powers over the earth and spirit world.

OTHER WORLD, THE—The dwelling place of spirits and ghosts. A euphemism for the astral world and other descriptions for the world immediately beyond the physical. So described for convenience and for fear of uttering certain words which may call the attention of the spirits to a mortal.

OUIJA BOARD—A method of obtaining messages from the spirit world. Varying in sophistication and ornateness, it is generally a board on which are printed the letters of the alphabet, numbers from zero to nine and such one-word answers as YES, NO, and MAYBE. Placed on a table or other flat surface, the board is operated by one or more persons, who place their hands or fingertips on a marker, called a planchette, which is then guided by spiritual forces to spell out messages of significance, to answer questions, and to make predictions. The derivation of the name is believed to come from the French *oui* and the German *ja*, both words for yes. In some remote cases, allegations are made that the planchette has been moved without human hands being placed upon it. In still other instances, as a supposed demonstration of veracity, messages are given in code, foreign languages, or in reverse.

OWL—In many beliefs, an omen of dread or impending doom. Among the Apaches of Southwestern United States, the owl is held to represent the spirit of a person who is able to enter the body of an owl to exercise an evil influence. They also believe the owl is able to give ominous warnings about relatives.

In other beliefs, a spirit which is seen and chased will frequently change into the form of an owl or bat before flying away.

P

PALLADINO, EUSAPIA—An Italian physical medium whose life began in the later years of the nineteenth century and extended into the twentieth, she was a handsome peasant woman who demonstrated psychic talents at an early age and manifested some of the most controversial phenomena known to psychical researchers. Many charges of fraud were leveled against her, charges to which she willingly admitted. An impish woman with a hearty sense of humor, she cleverly invented a showy brand of mediumship which bordered on the sleight of hand. But there was always a doubt, even in the minds of her most serious detractors, and her willingness to submit herself to some of the most strict precautionary measures produced only more bafflement. There is no question but that she played to her audiences, but in later years, in sittings with prominent psychic researchers, she managed to produce phenomena for which there were no apparent charges of fraud, nor were there valid explanations.

PALMISTRY—Divination by reading the lines and other markings of the human hand. It was practiced in ancient India and is still much in fashion in the contemporary world. The size, shape, and proportions of the hand, fingers and length of lines in the palm, as well as whether or not they appear broken, lightly or deeply etched; the mounts at the base of the fingers, etc. all have some influence on the reader's interpretations. Readings generally give past information and future prospects. The left hand is generally chosen for reading, and some palmists like to scan the back of the hand.

PAN—Literally all; the primitive force of Nature. As a figure, his upper body was human, but he had the legs and feet of a goat. His basic effect on mankind is beneficial because of his influence in keeping men from becoming too corrupt, artificial, and urbane, forcing man back into his proper place in Nature. The word panic means a literal fear of Pan; it is experienced especially in forests and woods where this extraordinary being dwells.

PAPA—In Polynesian mythology, the mother of the earth. Her consort is Rangi.

PARA—A prefix with Greek origins meaning, in occult definitions, past, beyond, beside, aside from.

PARADISE—The garden of Eden; believed to be located somewhere in the Near East. It is a concept prevalent in all folk myths of the peoples of the Near East as well as the Judeo-Christian religion.

PARANORMAL—An occurrence that is beyond the normal ken or the normal range of sensory experience, but specifically an occurrence that might, in time, have a scientific or reasonable definition attached as scientific progress and psychical research increase.

PARAPSYCHOLOGY—A study investigating by scientific means the psychology of phenomena which are apparently supernatural, i.e., clairvoyance, telepathy, apparitions, etc. This study recognizes the possibility of experiences beyond the normal range and attempts to define and explain the motivation for them, hence parapsychology would attempt to define the psychology of E.S.P. rather than present E.S.P. merely as an isolated phenomenon. The work of Dr. Joseph Rhine, q.v., has been particularly noteworthy in this area.

PARCHERO—In Mexico, a practitioner of magic, witchcraft, and healing. See also CURANDERO.

PAREGORIC—Camphorated opium tincture, a well-known elixir in medieval Europe.

PATH—An East Indian concept involving the way to God. See YOGA.

PEARLS—A part of the occult pharmacology. Often used in powdered form as an elixir or tonic, or to increase the amatory powers.

PEDOMANCY—Especially in China, a form of divination not unlike palmistry, in which the human foot is used.

PERSEPHONE—The daughter of the goddess of the harvest and the wife of Hades, thus she has a dual nature; a virgin goddess of sunlight and flowers, queen of Hell.

PEYOTE—(Lophora williamsii) An hallucinogenic used by the Indians of the Southwest United States and the Aztecs to obtain visions. To the horror of the Catholic Church, Christianized Indians in some cults refuse to give up their peyote ritual, which they link strongly with Communion and think of it in terms of being the flesh of God.

PEYOTE CULTS—Contemporary religious practices found among Southwest American Indians, involving a ritual use of the psychedelic drug for a communion with the mystical spirit of god, as a means of self-revelation and advancement; an admixture of Christianity and Indian animistic religions of the past.

PHALLIC SYMBOLS AND AMULETS—Because of its function in human reproduction, the phallus is a world-wide emblem of fertility and held to be sacred and filled with power and life force. Phallic amulets protect the wearer against the evil eye. In India, the phallus is the symbol of Shiva, the absolute god. In Africa, dried human phalli are considered to be potent medicine charms.

PHILTRES—A magical fluid which causes the drinker to either alter his behavior or physical appearance or health in a predictable manner. Part of the pharmacology of the occult.

PHILOSOPHER'S STONE—Actually an elixir believed by alchemists to have the power to transmute base metals into gold.

PHOENIX—In the mythology of Egypt, a bird of uncommon beauty which is said to live for over 500 years in the Arabian Desert and then consume itself by fire, rising from its ashes to begin another life cycle as a renewed, young, and beautiful bird. Often used by the Egyptians and subsequent religions as a symbol for immortality. Used also as a symbol of reincarnation and magic.

PHRENOLOGY—Divination by the configuration of the human head. The head was divided into areas which were believed to control a particular character or quality in an individual. The size of this area in an individual determined the amount of that particular quality he had, thus making it possible to arrive at a complex picture of the individual's nature. More or less a product of Franz Joseph Gall, a medical philosopher in Vienna, the science was introduced into America in 1832, where it had a widespread fame at the hands of Johan Gaspar Spurzheim, a disciple of Gall. It was adopted as a science by respected physicians on both sides of the Atlantic and at least anticipated certain physiological functions which are accepted today. Toward the end of the nineteenth century, it fell into disrepute as a result of hundreds of quack practitioners. Even today, it is not taken seriously among psychic researchers.

PHYLLORHODOMANCY—Divination with rose leaves; similar in function to reading of tea leaves.

PHRYGIAN CAP—The sacred cap of the Rosicrucians, q.v., also the ancestor of the mitre of all faiths. It is always red in color, peaked in shape. Its origin comes from the practice of circumcision, the cap symbolizing the tip of the phallus.

PISCES—In astrology, a sign in the heavens symbolized by a fish. See ZODIAC, HOUSES OF.

PLANATARY SPIRIT—Radiations from the absolute God, agents for creation.

PLANCHETTE—A heart-shaped slice of wood which is used as a marker in using the ouija board. In some cases, there is a pencil mounted to the planchette and it is guided by spiritual forces in automatic writing. Named for M. C. Planchette, a famed nineteenth century French spiritualist, who devised its use.

POISON ORACLE—A form of divination in which a substance is fed to an animal for the purpose of extracting a true answer. The substance may be poisonous. See BENGE. It may also have no effect. The death of the animal causes a verdict to be formed beyond doubt. The poison oracle is asked to inhabit the animal and kill it if the answer to a question is no. Then, for the purpose of corroboration, a second animal is used, the substance administered and the oracle requested to spare the animal if the answer is yes.

As an example: *First Test*—If X has committed adultery, poison oracle kill the fowl. If X has not committed adultery, spare the fowl. After first test, the fowl dies. Now, in corroboration, the *Second Test*—The poison oracle has declared that X is, indeed, guilty of having committed adultery. If this is the correct answer, spare this second chicken. And the sparing of the chicken by the oracle shows conclusively that X has committed adultery. The poison oracle is almost always used with two animals and asked for an answer in such a way that one animal will have to die. Both animals are given the same doses of the same substance, such as benge, which may or may not prove fatal to the animal.

Records of anthropologists show the oracle to work quite often.

POLYTRIX—An unlucky stone which causes baldness.

POLTERGEIST—Spirits which make noise, throw articles of furniture, upset objects, rap walls, and cause commotions. Almost all are, if not completely hostile toward men, filled with an impish spirit and determined to bedevil them. Some have been known to attempt to kill individuals or entire families by such methods as dropping lit matches in drapery, turning on the gas vent, placing pillows over the faces of sleeping individuals, etc. The subject of intensive investigation by modern psychic researchers, they are more often than not invisible. A growing theory holds that they are activated by the presence of girls between the ages of 12 and 18; some theoreticians going so far as to suggest that poltergeists are not spirits at all but telekinetic manifestations of these girls, which would suggest the girls have an unconscious or psychological motivation for hostility and mischief and manage to wreak havoc by mentally causing objects to move, etc.

POLYHYMNIA—In Green mythology, the patron of oratory and historical poetry. One of the nine muses, q.v.

POSSESSION—The state in which the individual's personality or body is invaded or taken over or controlled by a foreign spirit. In the case of a sensitive in the occult arts, this may be a voluntary situation with a resulting communication between the spiritual and physical worlds. This also implies the voluntary leaving of its host by the spirit. But there are records of possessions or alleged possessions of both sensitives and normal persons by spirits which refuse to remove themselves from the host body. A person thus possessed may die in fear of his soul being lost. Medicine men, priests, and shamans are frequently employed for spells and incantations in cases where persons or places are felt to be possessed. See also EXORCISM.

POSITIVE THINKING—A possible off-shoot of Christian Science, New Thought, and affirmations. Also linked with self-hypnosis in its goal of motivating and mobilizing positively directed physical and mental powers toward the accomplishment of a physical or spiritual goal, generally for a good purpose.

POULTICES—Hot, soft, moist, mud-like mixtures applied to an injury, either spiritual or physical, to absorb either the poisons or evil spirits dwelling therein.

POWDER OF SYMPATHY—An excellent example of contagious magic, it was believed that this powder, when applied to a weapon which caused a wound, would also cause the wound to heal immediately. Various formulas for the powder involve dried blood, skin, earth, herbs, spices, semi-precious stones, etc.

POWER—A psychic or occult force of effectiveness. See MANA.

PRASAD—Sacred food. According to Hindu and Buddhistic beliefs, God partakes of the spiritual substance of the food offered thusly to him. The "left-over" becomes powerful because of its contact with God and tends to make him who eats of it more holy.

PRAYER—Ritualistic communication to a god or deity, usually involving a request from the devotee, especially among mystics, also a chant of praise or devotion, or a recitation of the name and virtues of the god addressed.

PRECOGNITION—An awareness of an event before it takes place. The ability to prophesize accurately events which will take place in the future.

PREMONITION—An intuitional message in which knowledge of some future event will be imparted. Many humans are believed to have this capacity, but, according to occult theory, fail to develop it adequately by refusing to act upon these messages, thus destroying faith in them and the ability to receive them.

PRESS, A—An Amulet which is pressed down on demons, devils, and evil spirits while the magician chants: "I press down upon them in days and in months and in years and in this day out of all days." Used to vitiate the power of malevolent spirits and render their effects harmless.

PROPHETS—Usually a priest or occult adept who is given the ability to see into the future. The word is inaccurately applied to a diviner who uses physical means to read signs of the future.

A prophecy may be made through the unconscious medium's vocal cords, this in the case of trance; it may come directly from the conscious mind of the prophet as he recalls his divine vision or inspiration.

PSI—The human capacity for extrasensory perception.

The qualities already developed and those which are latent. Completely devoid of any mystical or magical connotations and used in the belief that extrasensory perception matters will become a full-fledged branch of science. Those qualities generally regarded as intuitive but which relate strictly to the reception of information and contacts which could not be made through any normal use of the senses.

PSYCHEDELIC—A form of drug often used in mystical and occult rites because of its alleged ability to expand the consciousness of the individual and increase his abilities toward mystical or religious experiences. A drug which produces hallucinations and thus, impressions which might be interpreted in a mystical or occult manner. See also LSD-25, PEYOTE.

PSYCHIC—A medium or sensitive; one who is susceptible to spiritual or occult possession or influences.

PSYCHIC BODY—The impalpable body; the spirit which is composed of attenuated matter and has the same shape but not the same limitations of the physical body. May be compared to astral body in the sense of freedom and potential.

PSYCHIC PHENOMENA—Manifestations of the existence of spirits, ghosts, astral beings, and worlds other than the physical. A form of behavior not subject to nor governed by the laws of chemistry, physics, etc. which govern actions of elements and persons according to science or scientific explanation, but specifically excludes all forms of behavior for which there is a potential scientific answer. For instance, a cure for cancer may be derived through psychic phenomena, but the cure is not, in itself, a psychic phenomenon.

PSYCHOKINESIS—A psi ability in which the individual is apparently able to cause objects to move by the strength of his will; the movement of objects by the exertion of mental force. Often abbreviated as P.K. See also LEVITA-TION.

PSYCHOMETRY—Divination of character by holding an object belonging to that person. The object supposedly exudes radiations of its owner which a sensitive medium may pick up. Peter Hurkos has been quite successful in assisting various police forces through the practice of psychometry, but care must be exercised in describing Hurkos' extraordinary talents, which also go beyond psychometry.

PUBLIC MAGIC—A form of magic generally initiated by a clan or group and channelled through the powers of a shaman, medicine man, witch doctor, cuarandero, etc. It is always directed toward the welfare of the group which performs or enlists it, but it may be malevolent in intent, used to bring evil or misfortune to other clans, groups or tribes. An highly powerful form of magic since the medicine man, etc. is assisted by the support and concentration of the entire group.

PYROMANCY—A form of divination based on fire and the smoke rising from it. See also FIRE.

Q

QUADRANT—In astrology, a natural division of the zodiac into three neighboring houses.

QUARTILE—In astrology, two planets which are 90 degrees distant from each other; an unfavorable aspect denoting the possibility of misfortune, hatred, disagreeable relationships, etc.

QUARTZ—Also called the eye stone, and used to make an

amulet which has healthful properties for increasing the vision.

QUASI-CONSCIOUSNESS—A state between consciousness and unconsciousness; a state of drifting where the dark is interspersed with spots of brightness. Psychoanalyst Carl Gustav Jung, many of whose theories borrow from occult principles, believed these bright spots to be the luminosities or sparks of the soul. Thus, a state in which occult power is being mobilized for a potential use.

QUETZACOATL—The Aztec god of the Sun and air; the feathered serpent god who wore brightly colored feathers to cover his ugliness. He was also the god of wisdom. Defeated in a duel of magic, he flung himself on a funeral pyre, promising, however, to return to his people if they should ever need him. He is still secretly worshipped in Mexico, particularly among the Indians who have been touched by Christianity but who refuse to give up this powerful practitioner of white magic.

QUICKSILVER—Also known as mercury; believed in medieval Europe to have magical properties because of its unique fluid properties and luminous appearance.

QUIMBY, PHINEAS PARKHURST, DR.—(1802–1866) An American physician specializing in healing and developing of healing properties and philosophies. Borrowing essentially from mesmerism and auto-suggestion, he was the founder of the New Thought Movement, q.v., and probably the first to use the term mental healing.

QUINTILE—In astrology, when two planets are 72 degrees apart. Considered a fortunate aspect, conducive to good relations.

R

RADIANCE—The apparent ability of some spiritual bodies to emit a glow. See LIGHT.

RAINMAKING—Magic for the bringing of rain is found in all arid and semi-arid countries. The Hopi Indians of the U. S. Southwest, for example, have elaborate rainmaking dances which, if performed properly, force the rain to fall. Other American Indians have ceremonies and dances in which the gods are offered gifts or told details of obedience. Primitives also make sacrifices of animals or burn food which they believe the gods will enjoy. Some more sophisticated rainmakers attempt to use a form of contagious magic, while still others go through elaborate preparations involving dry ice, static electricity, and burning various elements.

RAM, SIGN OF THE— An astrological sign. See ZODIAC, HOUSES OF.

RAMA—An incarnation of God. The hero-king of the Ramayana.

RAMAKRISHNA, SRI—(1836–1886) A semi-literate Vedantic mystic priest who believed encounters with God were possible and claimed to have had several. In some of these meetings or illuminations, he exhibited unusual physical behavior similar to the stigmata, q.v.

RAPPING—A noise of tapping or knocking, generally signifying the presence of one or more spirits. Usually an indication that spirits are attempting to give responses to questions put to them through the agency of a medium at a seance. But rapping noises are also characteristics of poltergeists.

Note that rapping differs from possession in that the

communicating spirits, whatever their purpose, do not use the human body as an agency, but rather manipulate physical objects to produce noises and sounds.

In the seance context, rapping is frequently associated with apports, q.v.

RAPPORT—A mystical relationship between two or more persons, usually a relationship of sympathy or understanding, but occasionally of antagonism. Witches establish rapport with those they hope to bring into the coven. Holy people similarly have the tendency to establish this mystical rapport with their followers. Thus, in occult terms, an especial form of agreement and communication. Particularly valuable as a concept for telepathic communication.

RAUWOLFIA SERPENTINA—(i.e. smoke root) A sacred plant in India, chewed by holy men to facilitate their meditations. Mahatma Ghandi chewed it regularly. Also used by East Indian homeopathic doctors and practitioners to soothe fretful babies and ease patients in cases of suspected possession. Reserpine, a powerful tranquilizing agent, has been found in it and is an active ingredient in contemporary pharmacology.

RED—The color red is identified with the planet Mars and projects the qualities of strength, health, and passion. Red is also the color of Satan and much loved by his followers.

RED CAP—A magical cap which, according to Irish belief, gave its wearer the power to fly.

REDEMPTION—The doctrine of Christian redemption is well known, but less familiar is the belief that ghosts associate with human beings in the hope of redemption. Thus an implication that the status of being a ghost carries a notion of purgatory.

REINCARNATION—The birth and rebirth of the soul in body after body, life after life, as a part of a pattern or system of development. There is an argument among believers in reincarnation in which there are two points of view. One states that the essence of the soul disintegrates after physical death and is completely reformed from the essence of other souls and godhead material before being introduced into another body; the other states that the same soul is reintroduced into a body and is thus capable of "storing" information which is useful in spiritual development.

In the latter, a well-developed enough individual may remember portions of a previous past life or all past lives, making it easier for him to advance to a plane of achievement where the soul may stop reincarnating and merge with the godhead on a higher level.

Most proponents of the reincarnation theory hold some regard for karma, q.v., and believe the soul is working off karmic debts and advancing itself in subsequent lives.

RELICS—Some part of the person, the clothing, or an object intimately connected with a deity or holy person. Hindus, Buddhists, Mohammedans, Roman and Greek Catholics all venerate relics as do many other religions and Satanic cults. The relics are believed to be invested with mystical or magic powers, either as aids in prayer or for the performance of miraculous deeds.

RELIGION—A system of philosophy, beliefs, and ethical behavior. It differs from magic in that the follower does not try to control nature directly, but addresses himself to intermediaries, gods and holy people, whom he believes to control and contain nature. It is these beings who supposedly intercede for the believer.

Mystical religion differs from usual religions in that mystics seek God for his own sake, seek to be with God or seek to become a part of the godhead rather than attempting to obtain God's help or guidance. See MYSTIC.

RESURRECTION—The return to life of a being who had once been dead. Distinct from reincarnation in that the body and soul revivify rather than undergo complete rebirth. The belief in this possibility of resurrection is universal and extends back into the dim past. Only the holiest of priests, the most powerful sorcerers, or the strongest magicians are reputed to be able to restore the dead.

The Irish and others believe that resurrection, although possible, is dangerous since it may bring a contamination from evil, thus bringing distasteful results and even disaster. Many religions believe in the time at which all the dead will be resurrected; these usually are religions which do not accept the probability of reincarnation.

Resurrected gods are focal points in Christianity, the Aztec and Egyptian religions.

RHABDOMANCY—Divining with the aid of a rod. Distinct from water witching, in this method of divination, a number of answers are attached to an object and the priest shoots an arrow at the object. The answer pierced by the arrow is the correct one.

RHAPSODOMANCY—Divination by opening a book at random and reading the passage which first strikes the eye. Rhapsodomancy is still practiced regularly by many, especially among Christians who use the Bible.

RHINE, JOSEPH B., DR.—American psychic researcher, particularly in the field of telepathy and testing for extrasensory perception ability. The most noted of his experiments is the use of an especially printed set of cards with four basic symbols. With the subject in another room, an assistant shuffles the deck of cards, then begins turning them up. The subject then attempts to "see" or "feel" through psychic means which card has been turned. Formerly associated with Duke University, Dr. Rhine has brought dignity, popularity, and order to modern American psychic research.

RHOMBUS—A ritual noise maker. See BULL ROARER.

RIDER ON THE WHITE HORSE—A famous European ghost who is seen in varying locations by many observers. The rider is always female and is an omen of impending war.

RIGHT SIDE, THE—The right side of the human body is considered lucky and is used exclusively in ritual offering. The exception is the Satanist, who traditionally considers the left side holy and who makes offerings with the left hand. From the Latin, left-handedness or left-sidedness is referred to as sinistral, hence the derivation of the word sinister from left.

RIGVEDA—A sacred Hindu text. See VEDAS.

RINGS—Because its shape is the mystic circle from prehistoric times, the ring has been used as an especially powerful amulet, both in religious and magical systems. Divinity, sovereignty, strength, power, unity, and protection are associated with the ring. The gods supposedly used rings for their own amulets. The Greeks believed that Jove invented the ring as a means of perpetual penance for Prometheus.

RITUAL—Ritual is to posture and movement what chants, incantations, and prayer are to speech. It is a series of proscribed and precise movements as a part of a ceremony. Especially with the practice of magic and to a lesser degree in religion, great importance is attached to performing the necessary steps perfectly. When this is the case, the ritual becomes the exclusive property of witch doctors or priests, who devote their lives to performing the set of movements. The word is frequently used synonymously with ceremony, but properly, ritual is a series of steps which comprise a ceremony. Thus, a rite is one ritual step.

RITUAL MURDER—Many religions and magical beliefs employ human sacrifice as a means of propitiating gods, powers, or supernatural essences. The ancient Aztec religion is perhaps the most dramatic example; here the sacrifice was performed with a jade knife. The incision is made over the chest, and the heart, still pulsing and dripping blood, is offered to the gods as proof of obedience and subservience. The Thugees, an Indian cult which worshipped the goddess Kali, believed in strangulation, but this was less ritual than the accomplished fact of offering the spirit of the dead as a token of devotion.

In some Mexican Indian cults today, ritual murders are still said to exist, and Catholic priests and missionaries are said to keep a watchful eye out against the practice since these Indians, and all primitive tribes which have seemed to adopt Christianity, are known to indulge secret practices of their former ways, modifying them at times to conform to Christianity, but deviating when the need arises.

ROSE—A flower which has been a mystical symbol of beauty, godliness, and power since the earliest of recorded times. The Greeks regarded it as an emblem of silence, a fact which so impressed the Romans that they coined the expression *sub rosa*, referring to the Greek practice of refusal to speak. Some mystics believe that a rose should be contemplated as a basis for further revelation. In occult pharmacology, rose oils, petals, and waters were essential ingredients in love philtres. Followers of Mohammed believe the rose had its origin in a tear, which sprang from the prophet's eye.

ROSICRUCIAN—A mystical brotherhood, still very much in existence and taking its name from the Latin *rosa* for red, and *crux*, for cross. The ancient symbol of the order became the rose, crucified in the center of a cross. The history of the Rosicrucian Order is shrouded in mystery and the exact date of origin is impossible to estimate with certainty, but the name was in circulation after 1600. In 1614, a document appeared in Germany entitled "The Fame of the Fraternity of the Mysterious Order of the Rosy Cross," addressing the learned in general throughout Europe and asking for an understanding of mysticism and the occult. Allegedly founded by a mystic and powerful magician whose name has come down only as C.R.C., the Rosicrucians believe there are secrets of life which are available to the faithful through study, ritual, and spiritual development. The older orders indulged in astrology, alchemy, healing, and occult magic. It has spread throughout the Western world, including America.

RULE—In astrology, a term meaning the association of a planet with a sign of the zodiac, q.v. For instance, the sign of Virgo is ruled by Mercury, which is the dominating planet of that sign; Taurus and Libra are ruled by Venus; Sagittarius is ruled by Jupiter; Aries by Mars.

The sun rules Leo, the Moon rules Cancer, Pluto rules Scorpio, Neptune rules Pisces, Saturn rules Capricorn, Uranus rules Aquarius, and Gemini is ruled by Mercury. Thus, the passing of a particular influence to a sign by a ruling planet. See ZODIAC, HOUSES OF.

RUBY—Worn as an amulet, it gives protection against witchcraft, pestilence, and famine.

RUYSBROECK—A fourteenth century Flemish mystic who believed that the soul maintains its personal identity even after it merges with God.

S

SACRED MUSHROOM—A psychedelic-containing fungus, used in religious practices among Mexicans, American Indians. See TEONANACATL.

SALIVA—Because of its intimate relationship to the body of the individual who produces it, saliva is believed to be a life fluid or substance, hence a belief that saliva contains the spirit of the individual. In contagious magic, q.v., the saliva is "treated" or "wounded" to heal or harm the individual from which it came. In sympathetic magic, q.v., saliva may be applied to a doll or effigy of an intended victim in a black magic spell. The saliva invests the doll with the life substance of the intended victim.

SALT—Has both prophylactic and therapeutic qualities in the pharmacology of the occult. Salt is believed to be sacred to the gods, thus its use to ward off evil since its presence is a constant threat to evil forces that a god may appear.

Heated salt is sprinkled on humans and cattle to prevent disease and a pinch of salt tossed over the left shoulder frightens away evil spirits which traditionally cluster on the left side of an individual.

SAMADHI—The state of being united with God; the goal of most mystics who also believe this goal may be achieved during the mortal life span. The Hindus and Buddhists believe it is the only way of escaping the wheel of life—karma—and avoiding the process of reincarnation. Samadhi is achieved through many different disciplines, but the descriptions from discipline to discipline are amazingly similar.

Also called ecstasy, union with God, illumination, q.v.

SAPPHIRE—As an amulet, worn to insure excellent health.

SARDONYX—A semi-precious stone which, worn as an amulet or drunk in powdered form, could protect the user from the adverse effects of witchcraft and possibly nullify some evil spells.

SATAN—The supreme deity of evil; originally an angel of God, but when he saw the dignities God bestowed upon man, he became jealous and rebelled. After a terrible battle, God drove the rebellious angel and his followers to Hell, where they still hold forth, devoted to removing dignity and salvation by God from man, practicing black magic and duplicity to obtain these ends.

SATANISM—The worship of the devil. May be a permanent alliance for the purpose of gaining black magic powers, or a temporary allegiance for the purpose of self-aggrandizement. In either case, the Satanic forces are said to have won.

SATURDAY—A day named after and ruled by the planet Saturn. A day with strong dangers of death and tragedy.

SATURN—A planet which exerts influences on men. See ZODIAC, HOUSES OF, and ASTROLOGY. This planet generally influences man to become knowledgeable, industrious, trustworthy, successful, and dignified, but may also have adverse effects in the more unfavorable combinations with other planets, as in the case of Saturday, q.v.

SATYRICA SIGNA—Latin for the sign of the satyr; an amulet in the shape of a phallus.

SCAPULAR—Two small pieces of cloth joined by strings, worn on the chest and back, under the clothes by some Roman Catholics as a sign of religious devotion. Also used in pre-Christian eras as a token of devotion to gods who granted protection from malevolent forces.

SCARAB—A beetle which lays its eggs in dung and therefore gives the impression that life springs from filth. Sacred to the ancient Egyptians, the scarab was their favored shape for an amulet, which then signifies the life force, eternal life and power with which to combat anti-life forces.

SCEPTER—Has something in the nature of a magic wand or rod which may command natural forces and objects. Also has amulet-like properties of protecting the owner from evil and mischievous spirits. Often used by a priest or medicine man as a display of power.

SCHMUTZLI—A companion of Santa Claus; an elf with a name which literally means dirty and offers hints that

Santa Claus has a dark side to his nature. Schmutzli is a punisher of evil and the King of Winter, but also an inveterate prankster possessed of a mercurial temper.

SCIENTOLOGY—An off-shoot and more refined development of Dianetics, a system devised by the American author and philosopher L. Ron Hubbard. Scientology is a systematic investigation of forces and events which decrease the ability of the individual to perform in a given area. There are emotional and pain-laden blocks called engrams which stand in the way of development. These engrams must be removed by a process known as auditing. An eclectic system for expanding the range of individual potential, and somewhat closely and variously allied to Christian Science, psychology, psychiatry, New Thought, and Self-Realization. Before the founding of these movements, Hubbard published adventure and science fiction stories.

SCORPIO—In astrology, a sign in the heavens represented by a scorpion. See ZODIAC, HOUSES OF.

SCROFULA—A common disease of the skin frequently cured by a laying on of the hands, particularly by English kings.

SEANCE—A convocation for the purpose of communicating with the dead or with the spirit world and presided over by a medium, q.v. Derived from both Latin and French words for sitting. A gathering of individuals who sit for the purpose of producing spiritual contact.

SECOND HOUSE—In astrology, a division of the heavens. See ZODIAC, HOUSES OF.

SECOND SIGHT—The ability to foresee events. Implications of the ability to have visions of future activities. Nearly obsolete now or considered as a colloquial to the more modern, precognition, q.v.

SEDNA—An Eskimo sea-goddess who controls sea mammals, sends misfortunes which are due to misdeeds committed by men. The Eskimo shaman must undergo a dangerous ordeal to reach her, then carefully stroke her hair, report the difficulties of his people, and offer contrition for past sins. The goddess listens, then gives a list of those who broke taboos. The shaman then returns from the sea goddess' dwelling in the ocean and gathers the people, who participate in a mass confession. At this point, Sedna returns lost souls, releases the game to run over the earth again, and cures all illnesses.

The trip is made by the shaman on behalf of one person or the entire village. Since this trip involves the ordeal of moving through the ocean and other attendant supernatural dangers, the shaman who performs it is considered most powerful, favored, and holy.

SEFIROTH—Ten numbers or principles from which came emanations of God, air, water, fire, and further emanations involving directions of right and left. These principles determined the content, while the 22 letters of the Hebrew alphabet determined the forms through which the entire matter of creation might be understood by the human mind. The sefiroth were first discussed in a book which appeared in Babylon sometime during the first century A.D. and which was believed to have been written by a collaboration of Abraham and God.

SELF—The personality, carrying with it the sense of identity.

SENDER—In the phenomenon of telepathy, the sender is the person who issues a conscious or unconscious form of communication. The impression is taken by a receiver. Sometimes mediums are spoken of as receivers. In spite of years of carefully supervised study, there is no apparent control over an ability to send messages which may be received telepathically, although it is widely believed now that some urgent purpose gives the message more impact. Often, messages or impressions of impending disaster are so powerful that they are readily received by even those persons who are not considered to be telepathic sensitives.

SERPENTINE—Cups made from serpentine increase the potency of elixirs and philtres served therein. Amulets made from this semi-precious stone protect the wearer against snake bite and poison. The porous nature is said to increase the ability of the wearer to absorb vile substances.

SEVEN—An highly sacred and mystic number. God rested on the seventh day. There are seven holy days in the Jewish year, there are seven sacraments, and the seventh day of the seventh month is holy.

SEVENTH HOUSE—In astrology, a division of the heavens. See ZODIAC, HOUSES OF.

SEEDS—Because of their generative natures, they were considered powerful as amulets. Inscriptions added to their abilities to aid restoration of health, lost wealth, lost powers.

SHIELD OF SOLOMON—A star formed by two equilateral triangles. See HEXAGRAM.

SIDEREAL BODY—The soul; the spirit of the person which is released at death. Commonly, the sidereal body is described as shining or radiating light and is immortal. See SOUL.

SIGNS OF THE ZODIAC—In astrology, symbols representing certain constellations. See ZODIAC.

SITTING—The act of being in or preparing for a seance and communication with the spirits. Used as a noun or a verb, thus sittings with famed mediums; sitting at a seance.

SIVA—The third phase of the energy of the godhead. Siva, male in characteristic, had many personalities and manifestations and on different levels of being. On the lowest of these levels, he is the god of the arts and dancing. On higher levels, he is symbolic of the destructive force of Nature. But on the most abstracted of all levels, he represents the godhead lost in contemplation of himself.

SIX—Regarded as an holy number because the creation took place in six days. Also important because it is the multiple of the first even number and the first odd number and thus involves a reconciliation of the two opposing forces of Nature.

SIXTEEN—Given a significance of strength, power, perfection, and unity because of the number of ways in which it may be expressed: 4×4, 2^3, $2 \times 2 \times 2 \times 2$, etc. In incantations and spells, the use of sixteen steps, sixteen incantations, or sixteen-sided figures was thought to be a perfect offering, one the gods could not ignore.

SIXTH HOUSE—In astrology, the house of sickness and servants. See ZODIAC, HOUSES OF.

SIXTH SENSE—Supposedly the next sense to be latent and awaiting development in humans after those of touch, smell, sight, taste, and hearing. The psi or esp ability, both of which see.

SLATE WRITING—A favorite medium for automatic writing, particularly if there is a large audience present. See AUTOMATIC WRITING.

SMITH, SUSY—American author, editor, newspaperwoman, psychic researcher. One of several lay authorities on the field of psychic research and psychic phenomena.

SOLIFICATION—In ancient Mithraic mysteries, this was interpreted as a mystical union with the power of the Sun. See SAMADHI.

SOMATOMANCY—A term devised by the American anthropologist William A. Lessa to denote the entire range of divination from the human body, including phrenology, chiromancy, and the various forms of astral physiognomy. In general, it is almost completely lacking from primitive peoples and found to an highly sophisticated degree in higher cultures which have long histories. There are two general forms; astral and natural. The astral somatomancy is more mystical, divinatory, and supernaturally oriented.

SORCERY—The use of supernatural power to control nature. The term generally implies at least a malignant magician if not a black purpose. This is in contrast to an alchemist, who is thought of as having a white purpose and who generally is not so choleric as the sorcerer.

SPARKS—Supposed emanations from the soul. See QUASI-CONSCIOUSNESS.

SPELLS—Incantations which force a person, group of persons, animal, group of animals, or an inanimate object to the bidding of the conjurer, magician, sorcerer, or alchemist. There are three basic types of spells; those which curse, those which cure and protect, those which injure and transform. Hence the expressions spellbound and under a spell. The power of spells is gained from the use of magical and often otherwise meaningless words, and from combinations of words. Thus a spell outlines the magician's intentions, powers it with a seed word or strong mana, or directs a god or supernatural force to combine the formula and produce the results. Abracadabrah, q.v., is one of many mana or spell words. Others are abranazukhel and mommon. See also HOCUS POCUS.

SPIRAL, THE MYSTICAL ORDER OF—An organization built upon eclectic principles and originated by Worthington Cake, an Irish occultist of the eighteenth century. Various elements such as wood, stone, metals, etc. were believed to have certain rates of spiritual vibration which could assist the adept at moving down the Mystical Spiral of Life and toward the vortex, which was a mergence with the godhead. Frequent cases of levitation, speaking in tongues, and other spiritual manifestations were reported. A series of incantations were built about the numbers 311, which were reputed to be the perfect numerical representation of a spiral.

SPIEGELSHRIFT—Writing backwards so that the result must be read in a mirror to be understood. Automatic writing is sometimes presented in this fashion and given in rapid bursts to serve as proof that the message is of genuine spiritual origin.

SPIRIT PHOTOGRAPHY—Attempts to photograph manifestations of spiritual entities or ectoplasm at seances. Thousands of samples have been offered as being actual photos of spirits, some reputedly of famed persons such as Houdini, Edgar Allen Poe, etc. In recent years, some attempts have been made to take such photos with infrared film and results have been obtained. But often there is not substantial evidence to warrant the conclusion that spirit photography is valid. In some cases, spirit photography is accidental; an innocent person develops a picture and finds he has caught spirits in addition to his intended subject. Because of the great possibility of fraud, such photographic work would have to be made under the most rigidly supervised of conditions to have any validity among psychical researchers.

SPIRITUAL BODY—The spiritual essence contained inside the physical body. See SIDEREAL BODY.

SPIRITUALISM—The system which upholds the belief in an existence of ghosts or spirits of the dead as beings which exist in reality as opposed to being hallucinatory phenomena. Continuation of life in spirit form after death as a belief or guiding philosophy.

Most existing knowledge about spiritualism comes from mediums or sensitives who are able to receive communications from spirits who wish to contact the world of the living. Although the main impetus of present-day spiritualism comes from the nineteenth century, similar beliefs and existing sensitives who received messages antedate history.

SPURZHEIM, FRANZ JOSEPH—A Viennese medical practitioner and probable founder of the movement known as phrenology, q.v.

STIGMATA—In the Roman Catholic religion, wounds symbolic of those suffered by Christ which may appear repeatedly in the same individual. There is often no medical explanation for the appearance of these wounds, which have included bleeding at the temples, bleeding at the feet, hands, sides, etc. Many cases of the stigmata have been recorded by the church and are generally investigated with exquisite thoroughness before being described as miraculous in behavior.

In general, the appearance of wounds or other physical manifestations such as scars, bleeding, markings. They will usually last for a set period of time, then disappear as quickly as they came.

SUCCUBUS—A demon who takes the shape of a beautiful woman for the purpose of seducing a human male. Some persons believe Lilith, Adam's first wife, was such a being.

SULPHUR—When powdered and mixed with water, wine, or molasses, this element was believed to be the basis of a strong elixir which protected the consumer against evil influences and fascination.

SUNDAY—A powerful day because of its relationship with the Sabbath in some religions. People born on Sundays are likely to be possessed of psi abilities.

SUPERNATURAL—Events and conditions which cannot be explained by the ordinary physical, organic, or psychological laws which describe known behavior. Events and conditions which may not be said to be hallucinatory in origin, yet which occur in conformance with rules and postulates as yet unexplained. Also used as a catch-all for spiritual and abnormal activities and beings.

SWASTIKA—A design in the form of a Greek cross with each arm bent in a right angle; one of the most ancient and powerful of amuletic signs. Pagan in origin, it is a fertility symbol in intent, but also becomes both a solar emblem and a sign of the female principle in Nature. See also CROSS.

T

TABLE LIFTING—A familiar form of psychical phenomenon exhibited at seances; a table is caused to rise from the floor, tilt and possibly rotate. The table is lifted by spiritual forces and may be accomplished with or without the medium's fingertips touching the table. Also a form of levitation which may be performed by a person not necessarily in a trance state and not necessarily in a seance.

TABOO—Literally a forbidden practice or ritual. Generally used in connection with mana; a person or object with powerful mana is to be avoided or approached carefully. A ritual which has strong mana attached should be avoided by persons of little or no mana. Also a violation of the word of a god or the violation of a magical ritual.

TAGES—Etruscan diviners who read the future in the entrails of animals.

TALISMANS—Objects which perform a specific magical task such as guarding a buried treasure, protecting an individual in one specific instance, protecting a country or home through one encounter with an undesirable force, etc. As opposed to amulets, talismans have a relatively short life span.

TANDRITANITANI—Among African tribes, the name given to a curse which is so powerful, the victim immediately accepts the inevitability of death, retires to his hut, and appears to waste away. Nearly always successful unless countered immediately by a strong charm.

TAROT—A form of divination with an especially marked deck of cards, 78 in number. There are four suits: grails, swords, wands, and pentacles. Each suit contains 14 cards, the ace, king, queen, knight, knave, and nine others. The keys of the Tarot are the emblematic figures which have occult meaning. Possibly, Tarot is as ancient as Egypt; it was and still is the basis of Gypsy fortune telling and has spread through the Western world. Tarot readings are said to be quite accurate, largely because of the deck being cut by the person who wishes the reading and because his touching of the deck imparts his own personality.

TASSELS—Ornaments which may be given mystical or magical significance. See FRINGE.

TATTOOING—Coloring the skin by means of subcutaneous ink injections; in occult practices, a means of turning the skin into a living amulet which cannot be lost or stolen.

TELEKINESIS—A psi power; the ability to move objects through thought power. Distinguished from all movement of objects by spirits. Persons possessing this ability are not necessarily telepathic nor possessed of mediumistic abilities.

TELEPATHY—The ability to communicate directly, from mind to mind, without the aid of normal sensory channels. Thus, the ability to transmit and receive mental pictures, words, and sounds which are as accurate and reliable as impressions sent via any other means of communication. Referred to as a psi ability and often mistakenly called mental telepathy, a term which is redundant.

TENTH HOUSE—In astrology, a division of the heavens. See ZODIAC, HOUSES OF.

TEONANACATL—The Sacred Mushroom, found especially

among the Chinantecs, Mezatecs, and Zapatecs of Southern Mexico. The active hallucinogenic ingredient is now known as psilocybin. Usual dosage is 15 mushrooms which produce fantastic visions, emotional excesses, and exhilaration. They are generally used as sacraments in religious ceremonies presided over by cuaranderos.

THEOMANCY—The study of divine mysteries; a part of the Kabbalah. Once mastered, theomancy gives the scholar power over angels and demons, the ability to see into the future, and the capacity to perform miracles.

THEOSOPHICAL SOCIETY—Founded by Madam H. C. Blavatsky, q.v., in the United States in 1875, its purpose was to promote investigation of mystic and occult knowledge. It teaches that all religions and religious systems have a common origin and truth. Of apparent Hindu and Kabbalistic derivations, the society accepts the doctrine of innumerable universes which were brought into being by the Logos, a word of God, a solar deity and a massive system of evolution, all of which are a part of God. Theosophists believe in reincarnation, karma, and samadhi, or the attainment of nirvana, q.v.

THEOSOPHY—A system of religious philosophy which claims mystical knowledge of the existence and nature of God and which is highly eclectic in nature.

THOUGHT READING—Telepathic reception; an indication of latent psi powers and possible ability to become an active "sender" of thoughts, impressions, sounds, etc.

THREE—A sacred number with alleged magical and mystical properties dating back to its inception. For the Babylonian, it symbolized birth, death, and life; for the Egyptian it was the implied essence of birth, death, and the spiritual world, and in Christianity is represents the mystic trinity of God, expressed as the Father, the Son, and the Holy Ghost.

THIRD HOUSE—In astrology, a division of the heavens. See ZODIAC, HOUSES OF.

THIRTEEN—In the pre-Christian era, 13 was regarded as a lucky number, but since the sitting of Christ with his 12 disciples, it has become the symbol of impending disaster.

THIRTY—An evil number, linked with betrayal largely because of the 30 pieces of silver paid Judas Iscariot for betraying Christ. Said to have limited power for summoning demons when expressed in Roman numerals.

THURSDAY—Named for the Scandinavian god Thor, overseer of battle, this day is an omen of courage.

TOBEY, CARL PAYNE—American author, editor, mathematician, astrologer. See *An Astrology Primer for the Millions.*

TONGUES—A spontaneous spirit message through a human agency, often in a foreign or ancient language. SPEAKING IN—See GLOSSALALIA.

TRANCE—An altered state of consciousness in which there is an increased susceptibility to the supernatural world and a corresponding decrease in awareness of the physical world. In this state, the mystic sometimes becomes completely immersed in the godhead or astral world and has mystical experiences or contacts with supernatural beings which either impart messages or wisdom to him.

The trance of the spiritualist or medium is more on the order of a clearing or momentary erasing of the consciousness so as to facilitate possession, q.v.

TRANSFORMATION—The changing of one being or object into another being or object. The Greek gods were particularly fond of transforming themselves, particularly for the purpose of begetting a child. Zeus transformed himself into a swan, thus the birth of his daughter Leda. Powerful witches also have the power to transform themselves into alien shapes and they may use spells to effect permanent transformations on other mortals.

TRANSMUTATION OF THE BODY—The magical belief that man might make use of a potion or elixir to restore himself to his primordial grace, beauty, strength, and immortality. A frequent quest of alchemists, for which they were often paid handsomely by an aging ruler or wealthy man.

TRANSMUTATION OF METALS—The use of alchemy to convert the baser metals into gold. See also PHILOSOPHER'S STONE.

TRAVERTINE—A yellowish marble worn as an amulet by children to protect themselves from fascination by evil spirits or from witchcraft.

TRINE—In astrology, a condition in which two planets are four signs or 120 degrees apart. Abbreviated as an equilateral triangle. See also GRAND TRINE.

TROLLS—Malignant dwarfs who dwell beneath the surface of the earth.

TUESDAY—A day influenced by Mars, bringing with it a tendency to quarrels, discords, and litigation.

TURQUOISE—A semi-precious stone, generally light blue in color and believed to be an omen of luck or an amulet of good furtune by the Arabs. It is equally prized by Indians in the Southwest United States.

TWELFTH HOUSE—In astrology, a division of the heavens. See ZODIAC, HOUSES OF.

TWELVE—Regarded by numerologists as an unlucky number, having especial effects on family or clan relationships.

TWENTY-EIGHT—A mystical number of especial power to systems and philosophies by virtue of its relationship to the lunar cycle. It is believed to be an aspect of the perfection of God.

TWENTY-ONE—A number of high magical properties because it is the multiple of three and seven, each regarded as perfect numbers. Originally symbolized majesty, power, and completion, in some cases this was extended to include the establishment of an enduring system.

At funerals of kings and nobility, 21 salutes were given as a final tribute, thus the modern tradition of 21-gun salutes at funerals or special occasions of state.

TWILIGHT WORLD—A euphemism for the astral world, so called because of the presence of shadowy figures and occasional luminosity which are found there.

TWINS, THE—In astrology, the sign Gemini. See ZODIAC, HOUSES OF.

U

U.F.O.—Unidentified Flying Objects, possible derivation, U.S. Air Force designation which has popularly come to mean any flying object, manned or unmanned, with extraterrestrial origin. Sightings of these have been recorded for several hundred years and are generally given little credence by the same persons who give no credence to current sightings. In recent years, U.F.O.'s have been reported in three distinct shapes, the flat, disc-like "flying saucer," the bell-shaped craft which apparently has protrusions resembling large ball bearings, and the tubular, cigar-shaped object which is allegedly quite large in size and reportedly a mother ship for the two other shapes. From the sightings and from persons alleging contact with the beings in the vehicles, they are operated on magnetic force.

UNGUENT—A salve or pasty potion, concocted by an alchemist for curing, charm, preventative, and bewitching purposes. See also OINTMENT.

UNICORN—A mythical horse-like animal with one horn

growing from its forehead. It could be caught by man for its magical abilities, but this capture involved placing a virgin in a field and waiting for the unicorn to approach her and rest its head in her lap. Hence, a test for virginity.

UNIVERSITIES, OCCULT—Numerous well-known centers of higher learning existed in medieval Europe; courses in the occult, magic, and alchemy were considered a part of the liberal arts curriculum. Similar universities were found in Egypt, Babylonia, Arabia, Greece, and Mexico. But these specialized in teaching the occult arts.

UPANISHADS—Mystical writings of the ancient Vedas; the earliest work extant in which the soul of man is viewed as a part of the infinite God.

UNITY—A mystical state implying a joining of soul with God. See SAMADHI.

UNDERWORLD—The world of the dead and of doomed spirits. Not all religious systems equate the underworld with Hell, but many tend to agree that this is at least a place of some anguish, a stopping-over place for tormented souls and for some malevolent souls still intent on the work of Satan.

UNIVERSAL BALM—A magic ointment that could heal all wounds and cure every sickness, restore every adverse spell. Distinct from the elixir of life in that it did not give immortality or even longevity except in the sense of curing a potential of premature death.

UNIVERSAL MAGIC—A powerful source of white magic, q.v., which may be called upon by the adept to do battle with black magic. Its use is not always completely effective and it may be the last resort in forcing a stand-off with black magic.

V

VACULATE—A practice of stealing the soul of a sick person to end an illness; practiced by witch doctors ranging from Alaska to Africa.

VALONIA—The acorn cups of the European oak tree (valonia oak), believed to be a magical cure because of the sacredness of the tree itself. An ink made from this acorn was also used for the writing of spells.

VAMPIRE—A person once dead, now reanimated to maintain a monstrous existence by drinking the blood of humans. Generally, the vampire makes an incision in the victim's neck using two teeth which have sharpened in connection with his vampire state. He drinks from the victim's jugular vein. Those whose blood he drinks also become vampires. Either sex may become a vampire; during daylight hours, the vampire must return to a coffin and remain in suspended animation, but after dark he awakens and goes forth seeking new victims.

VAPORIZING—Some witches were said to be capable of turning their physical bodies into a stream of vapor for the purpose of entering locked rooms, escaping their enemies, or spying on intended victims in a state of near invisibility.

VARUS—Literally bent-legged or crippled. In Europe of the Middle Ages, persons with huge moles on their faces and a crippled gait were considered varus, and thus no further evidence was needed to suppose their allegiance to Satan or witchcraft. They were subjected to trial by ordeal, q.v., or torture.

VEDANTA—The more abstract philosophy of the Hindu

139

religion. The word comes from Veda, q.v., but the Vedas are but one of the "Bibles" of Vedanta. The Upanishads and the Bhagavad Gita are perhaps even more important in detailing Man's relationship with the universe and God. Vedanta mystics are noted for their illuminations, or mystical experiences.

VEDAS—Literally books of knowledge; ancient Hindu scriptures written in Sanskrit. Probably over four thousand years old, they pre-date the Upanishads, q.v., and record the gods of India, the creation of man and his relationship to the natural and supernatural worlds. One particular Veda, the Regveda, addresses itself to a discussion of the interlacing of the natural and supernatural worlds.

VEGETARIANISM—The practice of abstaining from the eating of meat, sometimes even extended to include abstinence from those vegetables with roots growing downward. A common discipline practiced by mystics who believe the flesh of animals will vitiate their abilities to concentrate by causing them to think or feel in a manner that is too physical and worldly. As a temporary practice, witch doctors, magicians, and shamans, will abstain from meat before important rites as an act of purification.

VERDELET—An evil spirit who acts as master of ceremonies at the infernal court. He is also responsible for bringing witches to the Black Sabbath, or Witches' Sabbath.

VERGE—A magical rod or wand which is so powerful, it may cause enchantment. The verge is used in Christian ceremonies as well as in witchcraft.

VERJUICE—A powerful elixir used by witches to transform humans into animals.

VERMICULATE—An amulet for witches; a bit of wood which was grooved by wood-eating worms. It was worn to protect the witch from white magic counterspells.

VENESECTION—Cutting a vein, bleeding; one of the practices of medieval medicine and still an integral part of contemporary African witch doctor technology. The bleeding causes the evil spirits to flow from the body.

VETIS—An evil spirit which Solomon, through the aid of a powerful spell, imprisoned in a copper cauldron. The Babylonians unwittingly let Vetis escape. This spirit works directly under Satan and specializes in corrupting the souls of holy persons who are attempting to devote themselves to God. Also known as Veltis.

VIEDMA—A witch, q.v.

VISHNU—Part of the Hindu trinity of Brahma, the creator; Siva, the destroyer; and Vishnu, the preserver. He is believed to be blue in color, radiating a blue aura. His incarnations, Rama and Krishna, bore the mark of their godhead in their blue skins.

VISIONARY—A mystic, q.v.

VISIONS—The sighting of supernatural beings or scenes which are unavailable to mortals through normal sensory channels. Visions may be obtained through black or white magic, or through religious mysticism, and in each case seem to be accompanied by an emotional response which effects a permanent change in the spiritual personality.

VITALITY—Life force or pure energy, especially that which involves occult or spiritual ability. The life force of a strong person can feed a weaker person, that is, increase the amount of his life force. Similarly, there are magical means of tapping the energy which radiates from the godhead. Also believed by many mediums to be essential for conducting a seance. In this case, the force is analagous to powerful radio beams on which spirits may "home in" to make communications.

VODUN—A system of religion and magic which is practiced in Haiti and other West Indies areas. This system believes in divination through water gazing, card reading, and automatic writing. They believe sickness is caused by soul loss due to sorcery or spiritual possession. The evil spirit is driven from the possessed by bathing him with the blood of a freshly killed pigeon.

This system is closely linked with voodoo, q.v., and is another example of embellishments made by primitive peoples in an attempt to encompass their former beliefs with Christianity.

VOICE CALLING—Not a psi power of telepathic reception but a direct vocal spirit communication usually warning about an impending accident or disaster. Voice calling has also given warnings of other dangers such as bank failure, the approach of war, evil times, evil spirits, etc.

VOODOO—A supernatural cult which is particularly active along the African Gold Coast and the West Indies. In many ways similar to comparatively modern systems such as the Ghost Dance Religion and the John Frum movement, both of which see, some aspects of voodoo were based on a system to assure slaves an opportunity for a better life in the next world and a possibility of revenge against slave traders and cruel masters in this world. Liberally spiced with the belief in contagious and supernatural magic, both of which see, it is an eclectic supernatural belief, built also around Christianity. There are black magic aspects as well as white. The white aspects involve a closer approach to salvation through Christianity.

VOODOO DEATH—A generic term referring to death through curse and envoûtement, q.v. Verified accounts of such deaths are on record in Australia, the South Pacific, Haiti, Africa, Italy, and the Near Eastern Countries. Derived from vodun, q.v.

W

WAFER—A devilish wafer is used in the Black Mass to mock the Christian communion. Often, the devil's mark or his name is stamped on this wafer, which is then ingested in ritual and signifies the act of communion with Satan.

WALDER, PHILEAS—A notorius occultist who practiced witchcraft and satanism in the United States.

WALNUT TREE—A favorite site for a Black Mass, possibly because of the ugly dark stain walnut juice gives to the skin.

WALPURGISNACHT—The first night of May; the unholy night on which evil spirits, demons, and witches come forth for a revel and orgy, also to rob the graves and seduce unwary humans.

WANDERING JEW, THE—A legendary figure who, because he mocked Christ on his way to Calvary, was doomed never to die. The years have taught him repentance and given him the opportunity to learn occult powers, which he uses to help mankind in the hope that one day he will be forgiven and allowed to die.

WARLOCK—A male witch, with all the masculine counterpart abilities of a female witch, q.v.

WAR MAGIC—Variously culled from Africa, Australia, U.S., etc. A trident which, before battle, is ritualistically thrust into the head of a dead enemy is delivered to the medicine man along with the severed head. The head is added to a boiling pot of rooster blood into which all the warriors dip their spears. Also, a magical potion is made from rooster blood, redwood bark, oil, gourd seeds, and a type of banana cooked in a pot and given the warriors to eat. This makes them immune to injury.

In general, spears or weapons are dipped into a sacred solution which may also be applied to the skin of the warrior.

WATER—A symbol of life, growth, and goodness. Baptism and blessing with water are common to many religions; water is one of the few solvents witches tend to avoid. Water may be used as a part of a spell or ritual to banish or destroy a witch.

WATER, DIVINATION BY—Any use of water for oracular purposes. See HYDROMANCY.

WATER OF LIGHT—Any large body of water which flows, particularly river water. The Christians of St. John, also called the Mandaems, believed that river water has the power to renew the individual life from the Great Life. Another name for this cult is Maghtasilin, the washers or the baptists. They believe the accepted Christian practice of baptism by water taken from a vessel is ineffective because the water is "dead."

WATER OF LIFE—A translation of the Gaelic *usquebaugh*, which early alchemists believed was the elixir of life. The derivation of modern whiskey.

WATER SPIRITS—A mermaid or merman, both of which see.

WATER WITCHING—Detecting the presence of water sources under the surface of the earth by employing supernatural means. See DOWSING.

WATERING THE TOMB—A contemporary African practice which has origins in ancient Egypt; to please the spirits of the dead and renew their vitality, their graves had to be watered recurrently. Variations of "watering" involve the spilling of human blood over the grave or tomb.

WAX IMAGES—Because of their ready availability, wax and clay became popular means of assembling or moulding figurines of intended victims in imitative and contagious magic practices. Beeswax was believed to have even greater properties of magic because it was allegedly the anima substance of the animal kingdom. Some medicine men and kings made images of themselves from beeswax, believing these figures would increase their abilities at magic and their sexual stamina. But they lived in dread that these images would be discovered and used for black magic purposes.

WEALTH—Possesses a double symbology; it is a reward and a temptation, depending on how it is obtained. Both white and black magics have spells for obtaining wealth, but each has its own form of obligation for payment of the gift of wealth.

WEREWOLF—The power of some individuals to change themselves into wolves at specific times. As a curse, the victim cannot help but change into a wolf, in which form he is driven to perform specific tasks. See also LYCANTHROPY.

WHISTLE FOR RAIN OR WIND—The ancients believed whistling pleased the spirits who governed rain and winds and caused them to conjure accordingly. Still part of the modern sailor's superstition and paid lip service to by those who refuse to whistle on shipboard.

WHITE—A color which, in the Christian world, symbolizes life, purity, serenity, and virginity. But the more ancient symbolism is that of death. Ghosts are described as white, shrouds and winding sheets are often white and, throughout the Orient, white is the color of mourning. Generally speaking, the date and location of the use of white as a symbol will provide clues for the exact meaning, but in some cases, even occult and psychical research authorities admit to guesswork for interpretations. This is especially true in spells, omens, and divinations.

WHITE GOOSE FOOT—Literally a plant, but in symbol a person who causes bad luck and, although not harmed by it himself, a source of disaster to all who come in contact with him while he is under this particular spell or influence. Sometimes a strong spell, placed on particularly good persons by evil spirits.

WHITE LADIES—Malignant, supernatural beings who entice men to their death.

WHITE LADY OF IRELAND, THE—A banshee, q.v.

WHITE MAGIC—Any magic which is beneficial to mankind and in good intent. Generally, it is used to cure the sick and provide assistance in farming, animal husbandry, and with mechanical technology. Thus, dowsing may be the result of white magic. Occasionally it becomes a militant force, aggressively opposing evil. See BLACK MAGIC. In these cases, white magic will have killing powers, spells of invincibility, spells of protection, and especially endowed weapons.

WICKEDNESS—The supreme quality desired by Satan and his followers. Obedience to Satan.

WIGHTS—Beneficial spirits who are invisible to all those who lack second sight. They live in mounds, trees, and waterfalls. Offerings and respect must be offered them; if they were to leave, bad luck or evil may follow.

WILD WOMEN—Nature spirits who look like beautiful women and are very pious in their devotion to Christ.

WILD TALENTS—Psi powers, q.v. So called because of the belief held by many contemporary students of ESP phenomena that these powers are a product of evolution, coming from a "wild" or as yet unidentified gene. A theory that psi abilities are natural rather than supernatural.

WILLOW TREE—The devil's tree. If a person sits under a willow tree and loudly denounces God, the devil will appear and bestow supernatural powers which must be used for satanic purposes.

WISDOM, RELIGION, THE—Theosophy, q.v.

WITCH—A woman who possesses magical powers and a knowledge of spells, rituals, and incantations which harness supernatural and malignant powers. This knowledge is usually acquired through intimacy with evil spirits and granting of sexual favors to them. Often witches will have female apprentices whom they will teach spells, incantations, and sexual techniques. These apprentices are particularly valuable in seducing the innocent since they, not yet full-fledged witches themselves, may still have a greater appearance of innocence.

WITCHES' BANQUET—A Black Mass or Witches' Sabbath, both of which see.

WITCH CONFESSIONS—Confessions of malevolent intentions and pacts with the devil made by witches or their apprentices. There are two specific types. In the first, a witch will voluntarily confess her marriage to Satan, assuring her of death and the inevitability of salvation. The second is a confession extracted under torture or an assumed and implied confession when the conditions of trial by ordeal are not met. In some cases, an innocent woman is bewitched into making a confession in the belief that her soul may be snatched up at the moment of her death. In more devious cases, certain physical evidences of witchcraft are arranged, causing an innocent woman to be subjected to trial by ordeal.

WITCHCRAFT—Originally synonymous with the practice of any magic. Now taken to mean the practice of black magic with a strongly implied allegiance with Satan.

WITCH DOCTOR—One who practices magic, especially for cures, curses, and spells. Usually used interchangeably with medicine man, shaman, magician, and sorcerer. The terms are imprecise. Magician and sorcerer have fallen into disuse and a witch doctor should be thought of as being less sophisticated and religious in his orientation than a shaman. The witch doctor uses spells, incantations, herbs, medicines, fetishes, amulets, etc. to practice curing, healing, cursing, counter-spells, contagious and imitative magic. In more sophisticated cultures, a witch doctor will be a subordinate and often a rival of a shaman, who possesses religious powers. As another distinction, witch doctors may come by their trade through heredity, but are not bound to do so. Shamans almost always come by their trade through heredity. After several generations of witchcraft information being passed along, a witch doctor may be elevated to a shaman status. See SHAMAN.

WITCH FINDER—A person who uses his own supernatural ability to detect witches and betray them to the civil authorities of the community.

WITCH MARKS—Areas on the surface of the body which are insensitive to pain.

WITCH, SMELLING OUT THE—An African method of detecting a witch by means of detecting the faint odor of sulphur indigenous to the body or clothing.

WITCHES, TEATS—A wart or boil believed to be used by witches to suckle Satanic imps.

WIZARD—A sorcerer or male witch. Although most of the practices of the wizard are pagan, generally Arabic in heritage, the term wizard is archaic and now fallen into disuse with respect to occult and magical matters. Although wizards often worked for evil results, they were not considered to be in league with the devil, but rather they were rogues of great occult power.

WORDS—Certain words have great mana, q.v., just as some people, objects, and numbers possess it. These words are used in incantations, prayers, and spells. Words either have their own mana or are given power by a magician or priest who puts his own powers into them.

WORLDS—Planes or spheres of life. Theosophic dogma claims there are seven worlds: Divine, Monadic, Spiritual, Intuitional, Mental, Astral, and Physical; these in descending order of ability of those inhabiting them. These worlds are dependent upon each other, occupying the same space but giving up different rates of vibration and power.

WRAITH—The spirit of a person. Often used interchangeably with ghost, but semantically the terms differ in this respect; a wraith can be used to mean the spirit of a living person as well as the ghost of the dead.

WRITING OF HEAVEN—The term given by the ancient Hebrews to Phoenician writing because of the alleged magical powers it possessed.

WRITING ON SKIN—A variation of communications from the spirit world; words and even sentences appear in raised welts on the skin of the medium.

X

x—Used as a symbol for Christ, particularly because of the phonetics of the Greek letter chi, represented as X. Also, chi was believed to have mana. In pre-Christian eras, the symbol for a mystical kiss, then a physical kiss.

XANTHOS—The son of Helen and the father of Achaeus; thus similar in his legendary ancestory for the Greeks to that of the legendary ancestory of Isis for the Egyptians.

XENOGENESIS—Spontaneous generation of life coming from filth; a power of enchantment possessed by witches.

XENOPHANES—A Greek mystic, philosopher, and writer who believed, like the Vedantists believe currently, that life and change are illusory; only God is real.

XENOPHON—A Greek military leader who used medical sorcerers specializing in healing and surgery, particularly at times when war was contemplated.

XICIFU—The lucky period; the four months of the African Bavili year which were considered propitious times to begin new projects, plant crops, start new life.

XYLOMANCY—Divination by wood. There are several variations: the throwing of sticks in a manner similar to the I Ching, q.v.; reading of signs made by wood-eating (xylophageous) animals; divination by readings of woodpecker markings on consecrated trees; and, in Scandinavian countries, divination from the presence and juxtposition of sticks encountered on a forest path which has been chosen at random or recommended in a dream.

Y

YACATECUTLI—The Aztec god of merchants. His symbol was the cane or walking stick. He was propitiated by human sacrifice, and because of the importance of mercantilism in the Aztec economy, he became one of the most powerful, popular, and influential of their gods.

YADACHI—A Siberian conjurer who could influence the weather, thus controlling the movements of game and predatory animals.

YADAGERI—Siberian magic for controlling the weather. Snow and rain can be induced to fall or, more important, can be made to stop falling.

YAHWEH—The name of God. Perhaps the most awful, single and strongest element of magic found in the Kabbalah. Believed to be the name inscribed on the fore-head of the Golem, q.v.

YAGE—An hallucinogenic plant, known to have been in use for centuries by Amazon tribes in South America. Its active ingredient is now known as dimethyltryptamine, which is more powerful per volume than LSD-25. In group ceremonies, it is used as a means of divination and telepathy. The physical effects are increased motor activity followed by a state of drowsiness. Yage produces the blue halo effect, causing the user to be seen as having a blue halo, especially by another user.

YAKSHA—An East Indian fairy who capriciously helps or harms humans.

YAMA—The king of the Dead, a Hindu deity. Unlike Satan and Sith, both of which see, Yama is not malig-nant in character.

YAMAN—The desert tribes of Arabs who are the most mystical of all Mohammedans. They believe the prophet Allah dwells with them, in their tents, preferring their independence to the materialism of the city dwellers.

YANG—In the Taoist religion, the universal cosmic ener-gy produced the yang, a positive and male principle which interacts with yin, the negative female element to produce heaven, earth, and humanity. Thus a personal belief in the yin and yang principles within each indi-vidual.

YAZATAS—Nature spirits which generally attempt to con-ceal themselves from humans, preferring to provide beneficial services for growing things and for animals. Occasionally, they will provide some minor services for humans.

YELLOW—A color to be shunned because of its associa-tions with falsity and treason. Yellow as a symbol of cowardliness is of relatively modern origin.

YELLOW STONES—Worn as amulets, they supposedly

cured or prevented jaundice. In some cases, rather than wearing the stones as an amulet, they were soaked in water which was given to the patient to drink.

YEMENITES—Jews from Yemen who still practice the teachings of the Kabbalah and believe their ancestor was the Jew whom King Solomon imported to teach the son he had by the Queen of Sheba. The Yemenites cure by Kabbalistic amulet and philtre; they even have a special amulet to be tied about the neck of a cat, increasing the cat's abilities at mouse catching.

YGGDRASIL—A great ash tree of Norse legend, Yggdrasil extended three large roots, one to the land of mortals, one to the abode of giants, and one to a land of mist and rivers known as Niflheim. Next to each root was a well for watering purposes. It was believed that when the tree gave way, the universe would fall.

YH, YHWH—Abbreviations for Yahweh, q.v. Frequently used because the full name was believed to have so much power that it was dangerous to use.

YIN—In Taoism and other mystical philosophies, the female negative element which merges with yang, the male positive element to make the universe.

Y-KIM—A Chinese version of the Kabbalah, written at least three thousand years before Christ. The key to the Y-kim is a pentacle called the trigram of Fo-Hi, which is identical to the shield of Solomon.

YOGA—A path to God, thus a series of rites and beliefs which Hindus believe lead the follower to God. There are several paths, including the left-hand and right-hand paths, which generalize earthly and spiritual means of attaining union with God. Hindus believe there is no loss in status attached to the left-hand path, which is contrasted to the right-hand path of renunciation.

YOGA, BHAKTI—The path of love and devotion which leads the follower to God.

YOGA, HATHA—The path of postures or the physical path. In theory, Hatha yoga will lead directly to union with God, but in actual practice, it is used first to acquire occult powers for the enhancement of secular life.

YOGA, INGNI—The intellectual path to God which sometimes spurns the concept of a personal or anthropomorphic god and concentrates on union with an abstract God-force.

YOGA, KARMIC—The path of work. In this path, the aspirant remains on earth and continues with his secular life but dedicates each act to God. This is the path advocated by the Lord Krishna in the Bhagavad Gita scriptures.

YOGA, RAJA—The "royal" path to God by means of meditation or withdrawal of sensory perception.

YOGANI—A female yogi, very common in ancient India, but rarer in modern times when women are kept under relative subjugation.

YOGI—A male who practices one of the paths of yoga, usually under the close personal supervision of a holy person.

YORUBA HEALING CULT—A series of contemporary African sorcery groups which still practice ancient magic for healing purposes. By use of the occult pharmacology and by the laying on of hands or psychic surgery, they are said to be amazingly successful. Some sources attribute to them the ability to regenerate an entire human limb.

YUCATAN—The center of the ancient Mayan religion. Modern Mayans practice a curious admixture of their own pagan beliefs and Christianity. In addition to the usual spells and potions for illness, confession before a priest is required of every sick person. Some of the more adept are able to receive messages of divination from the spirits imprisoned in animals.

YURIPARI CEREMONY—A puberty rite of South American Indians in which the initiates drink a magical philtre consisting of potent doses of the psychedelic caap, q.v., then engage in ritual whipping until their bodies are covered with bleeding welts. Their ability to withstand pain and have ecstatic visions is said to influence their future medicine and occult protective powers.

Z

ZABULON—A devil who possessed one of the lay sisters at the shrine of Loudon; a disincarnate body who attempts to feed on pilgrims who visit shrines.

ZAEBOS—A dignitary of the lower regions; a demon with a human head and the body of a crocodile.

ZAHURIS—Spanish sensitives and telepathics who have the power to see water and minerals under the earth and to read minds and closed books. Only those persons born on Good Friday can become Zahuris.

ZARATHUSTRA—A Persian religious leader. See ZOROASTER.

ZELEM—A Hebrew word for the image of God in which man was created. The Kabbalists believe that the truly advanced occultist may see this zelem and thus have a glimpse of God.

ZENO—The author of a terrible exorcism for disease; methods of curing which are so unpalatable they are often referred to as Zeno's curse and as black magic. Zeno's approach was the use of dismembered animals, blood, and other materials. His favorite curse was, "A filthy, false, flattering, fallacious, foul, fickle, felonious, forswearing, foolish, fornicating, flatulant fiend."

ZODIAC, HOUSES OF—Divisions of the heaven into twelve areas through which the sun and other planets move in various relations; the basis of astrology, q.v. A horoscope is a map of the houses of the zodiac, noting the exact positions of the planets in various houses at the time of an individual's birth. The houses have signs, ruling planets, and various characteristics attached to them.

The first house of the zodiac is the house of life and the personality of the individual. Aries is its ruling sign.

The second house is the house of material possessions and man's acquisitive nature. Taurus is its sign.

The third house represents ideas and some intellectual activity. Gemini is its sign.

The fourth house is representative of home and security and is ruled by Cancer.

The fifth house involves service to one's self, family, profession, etc. It is also the sign of children. It is ruled by the sign of Leo.

The sixth house is related to body, mind, general well-being and health. It is ruled by the sign of Virgo.

The seventh house is the area of marriage, love and family relations. Its sign is Libra.

The eighth house is the sign of death and of spiritual responsibility. It is ruled by Scorpio.

The ninth house is the area of learning, religion, science, and communication of ideas. It is presided over by Sagittarius.

The tenth house is the house of honor, ambition, and community standing, ruled over by the sign of Capricorn.

The eleventh house is the area of friends, love, loyalty, and the maturing of the individual. This house has Aquarius as a sign.

The twelfth house is the area of enemies, deceits, and abuse; in a sense it is an influence of retribution and it is governed by the sign of Pisces.

ZODIAC, SIGNS OF—The twelve signs of the zodiac are:

Aries, which is in effect from March 21 to April 19; it is indicative of a fiery, masculine, violent, and commanding personality. It has been called the sign of the ram.

Taurus, the sign of the bull, extends from April 20 to May 20; it is representative of a cold, earthly, feminine, and nocturnal person.

Gemini is often called the sign of the twins; it extends from May 21 to June 21; its natives are restless, active, and often nervous, reflecting the influence of the planet Mercury.

Cancer is the natural fourth sign of the zodiac. It is the sign of the crab and extends from June 22 to July 21.

The fifth sign of the zodiac is Leo, the lion, extending from July 22 to August 21.

Virgo is the sixth sign, extending from August 22 to September 22. This is the sign of the virgin, ruled over by the planet Mercury.

Libra is the seventh sign, often called the sign of the scales. It extends from September 23 to October 22 and is ruled by Venus.

Scorpio, the sign of the scorpion, is the eighth sign of the zodiac, extending from October 23rd to November 21.

The ninth sign is Sagittarius, extending from November 22 to December 21 and ruled by the planet Jupiter. It is called the sign of the Archer.

The tenth sign is Capricorn or Capricornus, the sign of the goat, extending from December 22 to January 20; it is ruled by the planet Saturn.

The eleventh sign is Aquarius, the water bearer, which is influenced by the planet Uranus and extends in time from January 21 to February 19.

The twelfth sign of the zodiac is Pisces, the fishes, extending from February 20 to March 20. It is influenced by the planet Neptune.

ZOHAR—A book of hidden doctrines which is regarded as the most important book in the Kabbalah, q.v. It tells of an eternal radiance which originated all creation and all the forces of creation.

ZOROASTER—A Persian religion which centers on the struggle between good and evil as symbolized by the conflict between light and darkness. In effect approximately one thousand years before Christ, it was the religion followed by most Persians before their conversion to Islam. A strong belief in afterlife.

ZRACINE VILE—Spirits which are enemies to man; they tease when feeling benign and may kill when ill-tempered.

ZUGARRAMURDI—A famous seventeenth century witch cult which met in a large cavern into which flowed a river called the Stream of Hell. The cult contained; (1) children taken by force, (2) children who consented to be taken, (3) older novices who were about to denounce God, (4) neophytes who had already renounced God, (5) makers of spells and poisons, (6) teachers, (7) senior sorcerers and witches.

OTHER LIVES
Brad Steiger and
Loring G. Williams

Have *you* lived before? Startling case histories of
people who claim reincarnation, with documentation
and transcripts.   A518—75¢

THE MEANING OF YOUR DREAMS
Franklin D. Martini

The complete dream dictionary! Over 900 listings
help you analyze each night's dream.   A573—75¢

LIVING WISDOM FROM
THE WORLD'S RELIGIONS
Edited by George L. Abernethy

365 daily readings--a joyous selection of poetry, wisdom and prayer drawn from every major religious
tradition,. both East and West.   A587--75¢

YOUR BIRTHDAY
Stella,
Nationally Syndicated Astrology Columnist

Completely unique! An astrological guide based on
your *day* of birth, with forecasts and character analyses
as personalized as your fingerprints.   A563—95¢

THE POWER OF FAITH HEALING
Shaw Desmond

Revealed—the secrets of the great healers and their
magical cures. You could be a natural-born faith
healer unknown to yourself. Find out in this amazing
book.   A533—75¢

Mankind's oldest mystery—immortality through...

REINCARNATION
Hans Stefan Santesson

You might have been a Roman centurion—or a Renaissance artist—or even a French revolutionary.

Perhaps you marched in the Great Crusade, advised the Emperor of China, or recorded the history of Greece...

Impossible? Read this book! It will help you discover the many fascinating facets of your previous existence—by demonstrating the ancient methods of Recollection, methods that help you cross the boundaries of time.

And, even more amazing, now you may gain access to the darkest mystery of all—*who you will be in lives to come...*
A482—75¢

THE UNDER-PEOPLE   *Eric Norman*

One of the most provocative books of the year! Amazing, documented facts about the bizarre inhabitants of the center of the earth.   A545—75¢

FLYING SAUCER INVASION: TARGET--EARTH
Brad Steiger and Joan Whritenour

From experts in 40 countries—brand new, fully documented evidence of UFO hostility, contact with humans, landing in populated areas, and other fantastic saucer sightings.
A506—75¢